It All
Begins With
" I "

It All
Begins With
" I "

The
"New Rules of Thinking"
and the
Simple Secrets
to living a
Rich, Joyous,
and
Fulfilled Life

STUART K ROBINSON

Tallfellow Press
Los Angeles

Tallfellow®Press
Los Angeles

Published by
Tallfellow® Press
9454 Wilshire Blvd.
Beverly Hills, CA 90212

Visit www.Tallfellow.com
and
stuartkrobinson.com

ISBN 978-1-931290-05-0

Printed in the USA

10 9 8 7 6 5 4 3 2 1

For Nikki, Ally, and Leslie...
in my small effort to build you a better world.

To Maureen... for building mine.

TABLE OF CONTENTS

PREFACE

It was a stunning and unforgettable moment. One of those moments you wait your entire life to witness. It was completely unplanned, without design, and in truth, a moment that could easily have passed without being noticed. But through the sheer good fortune of the fact that I was able not only to notice it, but to be struck by the powerful universal truth of the moment, it was transformed into a life-changing event for which I will be eternally grateful.

The fact that I was celebrating a birthday is only relevant in that I think we all tend to be a bit more reflective on birthdays, and therefore perhaps our "antennae" are up looking for meaningful signals. Or maybe just the fact that we're often surrounded by loved ones opens our hearts in a way that allows for a deeper appreciation of new concepts.

Whatever the case, I found myself gazing at a cake covered with a shocking number of candles. (Could I really be that old?) And, of course, someone shouted instructions to "make a wish" before blowing my birthday breath all over the cake about to be divvied up between the guests.

At that moment I thought to myself, "What do I wish for? If I could have anything in the world, what would I want?" This was a difficult moment. For me, a classic overachiever whose passions and interests have always tended to be dizzyingly diverse, the first instinct was to avoid wishes altogether lest I bore my guests with silence as I pondered the various considerations. I had already spent wonderful yet challenging years in the Entertainment industry, acting, directing, writing, composing, and working in casting and talent agencies. Being a husband, father, friend, business executive, author, keynote speaker, life coach, and other myriad titles — is this nuts or what? — how could I settle on just one birthday wish? What could I possibly choose?

And, incredibly, the answer came back... nothing. Nothing more.

There is nothing I could wish for that I don't already possess. Obviously I could wish to win the lottery. But what would that bring me besides money, which I've already been given the ability to earn? Granted, I'm not a multimillionaire, but I have what money I need, and the means to acquire more if I so choose. Besides, studies show that an overwhelming majority of the people who win the lottery find themselves less happy than before their winning ticket was cashed.

What else could I wish for when I have a loving wife, two intelligent, beautiful, healthy children, supportive friends and family, a comfortable home, the car of my dreams, and, frankly, the freedom and resources to go out and get anything else that I desire? I could wish for longevity, but I currently have my health, and see no reason it won't continue.

More importantly, I have the New Rules of Thinking.

I've been blessed to have a few simple keys revealed to me that reinforce the reality that most anything is not only possible but within our control to manifest.

It's not magic. It's not mystical or religious, although you are welcome to appreciate it as magical if you like, or to attach any theological significance you feel is appropriate. It's not any kind of noodleheaded hocus-pocus, rather simply some fundamental revelations and guidelines to help you through the trials and tribulations of modern-day life. I am not preaching these "rules" from a soapbox, a mountaintop, or an infomercial soundstage. I am simply sharing the wealth, hoping you will apply these concepts to find the success you truly deserve, and find yourself in front of a cake filled with lighted candles celebrating the fact that there's nothing more in the world you could wish for than the continuation of your personal power to use these New Rules.

And the truth is, if you really felt happiness and success were yours unconditionally, I believe you, too, would find nothing to add to your birthday or wee-hours-of-the-morning wish list. I'm not talking about a one-time, rub-the-magic-lamp, miraculous-granting-of-a-fantastical-wish. I'm talking about "knowing." The unshakable knowledge that by simply including some fundamental concepts in your daily approach to life, your happiness, your success, and the experience of your precious and unique existence are yours to control.

So, what did I wish? I wished for the ability, the channel, and the privilege to share this new way of thinking with a large number of people, to give others the chance to make use of 14 fundamental guidelines that empower every person to shape a fulfilling, prosperous, and joyous life. To pay it forward, if you will. And once again, I've been blessed because these pages are the realization of that birthday wish.

It is my pleasure to offer these ideas, and a personal joy that the only wish I'll have on my next birthday is that millions more people will pay forward my sincere wish.

INTRODUCTION

What is your deepest desire? What do you really want?

Probably the same thing most others really want: a happy and fulfilled life. When we don't experience life as happy and fulfilled, our tendency is to look for someone or something to blame, our parents, our boss, the government, an adversary, and a lengthy list of others. However, even if and when we identify someone to blame, we are struck with the stunning truth that we have zero power to change those people or conditions. And so, we feel powerless.

That feeling stops now.

In the pages that follow, you will see that you have all the power you need. You have the power to change the only things you actually can control — yourself and your point of view on every event and every moment of your life. And when you take control of and adjust that point of view by understanding and steadfastly following the New Rules of Thinking in this book, you will see miraculous results.

These guidelines, the New Rules of Thinking, are not completely new ideas; they are concepts you might already know. You simply might have failed to remember them in the heat of battle of day-to-day life. Or you may not have accepted them as "rules," which conveniently allows you the freedom to use them sometimes and ignore them other times… which seldom works when dealing with rules. Perhaps, sadly, you've lost faith there is any true path to success and have come to believe prosperity of any kind is reserved for other people. In any case, you may just be in the right place at the right time to absorb the New Rules of Thinking. If you embrace these concepts as the rules of your existence, you will be able to control the amount of joy, success, and satisfaction you have in your life.

In other words, you will singlehandedly change your own destiny. How do I know it works? Every moment of my life and the lives of others with whom I've shared these principles is a constant shining reminder of the power each of us is given at birth. I say "reminder" because while many of these concepts may be familiar to you, I've gathered and organized them into a comprehensive, easy-to-digest rule book that, when followed, will prove to be life-changing. As you read, very quickly it will become evident that the concepts in different chapters overlap. Those similarities are intentional because the truths within these pages will work synergistically. No one New Rule of Thinking is meant to be employed without the others. They are designed to collectively address different aspects of your journey. You may have to review some of the pages many times to see the connection to your own path, but I am confident you will see that these commonsense, authentic observations can become the gateway to your happiness and success.

When faced with a serious dilemma, you can utilize New Rule #4 to find a unique and creative solution to your problem.

When the challenge is your own confidence or self-esteem, you might apply New Rule #6 to quiet the doubting voice in your head, replacing it with a supportive and visionary "coach."

When your frustration with family, friends, or co-workers reaches a boiling point, New Rules #7 and #9 will offer the tools to allow those people their eccentricities while you practice a new and powerful empathy that will give you peace of mind and clarity.

In nearly every interaction of your life, you will find essential value in utilizing these simple yet instrumental guidelines. In short, these New Rules will remind you to employ your best life strategies. And when you activate these strategies, the joy and reward you desire will surely follow.

Why should you have prosperity? Do you need a reminder? Please take a moment to remember this fundamental truth:

Happiness is your birthright.

You certainly were not put on this earth to suffer and struggle. Happiness and success are yours to claim.

Yes, life is tough, and the path is confusing. Not every day will feel ideal. That's why you need useful rules to get you on the right path, to keep your spirits aloft, and to continually remind yourself of what a wonder you are, and how fully you are intended to have the life of which you dream. Some say life is a game. If this is true, we all need a set of rules in order to play it to the best of our abilities.

Suppose someone told you right now that there would be a fantastic prize if you could only win the next game of... "Blitzball."

Ready... ? Go!

How could you win? You don't know the rules! You don't know how points are scored, or even *if* points *can* be scored. You don't even know what Blitzball is! So, what can you do but run around creating activity in the hope you will do *something* that makes you a winner?

Life can be much the same way. It's time to cease the exhausting, meaningless, hope-good-things-happen activity, and remind ourselves of the rules... the New Rules.

Read on. We're going to play a game of happiness, prosperity, and fulfillment (with a fantastic prize).

Ready...? Go.

Think of this as the beginning.

— The author

"I"

You can't change the game, but you can change the rules… your personal rules. You can construct a new set of options that govern how you will react to and interact with others, as well as how you view and treat yourself. Together, let's create new standards by which you will conduct yourself, and thereby transform the way you experience each moment of your life. Think of it as a new set of tools that will allow you to shape the future you desire. That is, after all, what tools are for, right? With all the skill in the world, a carpenter can't really build a table without the proper saws, drills, sanders, nails, and more.

Here's an important distinction: Without these tools, is he or she less of a carpenter, less capable, less worthy of respect? No, simply a carpenter who can't create a table today. Many of the people I work with are under the impression they are not good at what they do because their results do not reflect the success they desire. Often, it doesn't take much time to reveal that each person has been attempting to achieve results without the proper tools… or with no tools at all… a carpenter who wonders why the table couldn't be built with just bare hands.

You need tools! Imagine a pianist holding a recital in a large venue with a huge audience, a terrific sound system, immaculate lighting… and no piano! How would that work? It wouldn't.

My New Rules, used properly, will serve you in the same way a carpenter's hammer becomes an invaluable part of the daily routine.

Do we really think the creation of a coffee table takes less tools than the shaping of a successful life? Seriously?

If you'll accept these rules as tools, and strap them on, we just might get some serious work done. Please, don't show up to work and leave your tools in the car. Make the plan to learn and embrace them, and promise to use them every day, every hour, and every minute. If you don't, they really aren't rules or tools, are they? So, let's get to work with these tools right now.

We'll start by creating a new language to go with our New Rules. Let's refer to yourself as "I." Think of "I" as the best part of you, the most noble, most powerful, the most deserving and welcome on this planet. "I" is the enlightened part of you that is dedicated to creating the most beautiful, most rewarding, most productive, most loving existence possible. "I" creates a life in which you contribute thoughts and deeds to the world that will ensure a lasting and positive legacy.

"I."

We got a little clever with the title *It All Begins With "I."* Obviously, "it" starts with the letter I. Hilarious, right? But go deeper. If "it" represents your life, your dream, what you feel day-to-day, and the "I" is the one who shapes this journey, then it truly *does* all begin with "I." It bears repeating: You have very little power over your boss, the government, your significant other, your neighbors, or any of the other billions of people inhabiting the earth, but you do have the ultimate power over yourself and your reaction to every moment of every day. If the journey you're on is not the one you desire, and you want to change it, you have to begin by changing "I."

Every decision you make, every action you take, moment-to-moment, builds the life you will lead. That is how powerful you are in constructing your life. Take a moment and imagine what would happen if you knowingly created actions, feelings, and beliefs designed to enhance and electrify your experience of this life. You have the power.

2

Let's be clear — you don't have the power because you're so great, because you're so special, because you're more deserving than other human beings. You have the power because it's *your* dream. As a result — I must repeat — you have very little power over me, your neighbor, or the cashier at your local grocery store, but you have *absolute* power over yourself — and your perception of each moment.

The good news is, if this life is a product only of our perception — it is changeable. Why? Because when each moment is subject to the interpretation of the participants, there can be no absolute truth — only what you think, and only what you feel. Therefore you shape it by taking control of your perspective, your reactions, and your feelings. *Your* truth. Your dream.

I get it. For some, this is all sounding way too touchy-feely. "I am the master of my dream." Blah, blah, blah. "I've heard it before." Okay. Let's get out of the touchy-feely and into the… well… touch and feel. Real stuff you can wrap your head and your emotions around.

Right now, smile. For no reason, just smile. Notice how simply showing your teeth comes with a feeling slightly different than the one before. It may be subtle, but it's different. Now, if you choose to magnify that feeling, to trust it, to believe it, it would impact the next thing you feel and the next thing you do. We don't have to get all metaphysical to grasp the concept that whatever you're feeling right now is your choice. Are you enjoying the act of reading? Are you confused? Does your confusion cause you frustration? Or does it intrigue you, making you excited to solve the puzzle? It's your choice. Hey, only for a minute… be very serious. Process these next few sentences in as serious a mood as you can. Look how the feeling that followed the smile of the moment before has now changed to something else. Not better or worse, just different — a result of your choice. You're in charge.

So what do we do with all of this power? It's a huge responsibility. It certainly is a lot easier living with the idea of external forces and other people controlling our destiny. That way we are only a shiny metal ball bouncing around the pinball game of life, batted here and there, reacting to each person, place, and thing we bump into. No responsibility, no control. Our experiences and our results will only be as good as the person tapping those flippers on the side of the machine.

But if you want change, it all begins with "I," and with the adjustments you make **internally**: your world view, your actions, and most importantly, the way you view yourself. And therefore, you must accept the responsibility that comes with it, just as you will accept the bountiful rewards this change will create. You need guidelines, kind of like an owner's manual — or in this day and age, a "help" tab — that pull-down at the top of your computer screen. That's where the New Rules of Thinking will come in very handy. Whenever you are in doubt and could use a little guidance on how to move forward in the direction that will make the most of every moment of your life, keep these New Rules handy. These New Rules will not change your life. This book will not change your life. You... "I"... will change your life. Whether you like it or not, you're changing your life as you read. The question is, are you changing it in a way that creates a pathway to the things you want most?

There's an old quotation: *"Events don't change lives; decisions do."*

Let's use the New Rules I'm about to share with you to help you make decisions that serve your highest interests, goals, and dreams. I know, the minute you start talking about dreams, people around you begin to roll their eyes, as if dreaming was something to be ashamed of. But you have to believe me; it's *all* a dream.

What kind of dream will it be for you? It's your choice. It's up to "I."

It all begins with "I."

Mistakes are the portals of discovery.

— James Joyce

NEW RULE OF THINKING #1:

I Will Take Every Rule I've Ever Been Told That Includes "Don't" Or "Never"... And Add The Word "Badly" At The End

That's the rule.

Follow it.

The truth is, you can do most anything you want if you do it well, and to positive effect. It's only when you do it badly that it becomes a problem and hence the "rule."

Throughout my career as an advisor and a life coach, I have found most of the advice my clients have received from other "experts" centers around the words "don't" and "never."

"Don't" is certainly a useful concept, reminding us to steer clear of dangers and difficulties that may cause us harm or set us back. But what use is it in guiding us to success? It focuses only on what *not* to do, while leaving out instructions on what is actually necessary to prosper.

Right now, wherever you are, for one minute try *not* to think of a pink elephant. I mean it; don't you dare think about pink elephants!

Well, if you're like most people, the mere suggestion of said pink elephant brought all kinds of immense dancing ivory-tusked pachyderms into your thoughts, and the "don't" instruction merely

7

served to place your focus even more distinctly on… elephants… pink ones. If instead, you had been given a direction of something else to positively concentrate upon, elephants would never have come into the picture. So, when you accept advice with "don't" attached, you are usually only drawing that thing you wish to avoid even closer to you.

Why, I ask you, when seeking advice would you be interested in someone telling you what *not* to do? Was there ever a more defeatist approach to success than focusing on what you *don't* want to do? Any expert worth his or her salt would admit that acting from a negative point of view is the worst possible course of action. Can you imagine the result if a pro boxer is concentrating on *not losing?* Would the trainer ever shout from the corner of the ring, "Don't lose!"?

In this hypothetical boxing match, how would advice on what *not to do* be of any use in helping you defeat your opponent? Sure, it will help you avoid getting your head knocked off, but did you really need rules or advice on that? *"Hey, don't get your head knocked off."* Thanks, coach, I think that's a given.

As a result, I am of the belief that in place of advice about what not to do, and what never to do, you should be in the market for advice on what *to do.* My motto is: *don't tell me how to avoid disaster; tell me how to achieve success.* I want to know what it is I need to do *to* win, not how to make it to the twelfth round without making a fool of myself, not how to endure an investment that ultimately breaks even, not how to uneventfully sustain a relationship that is unfulfilling. No thanks.

A number of so-called experts will lay a whole bunch of warnings and don'ts on you, calling them "the rules," which does little more than trigger your fear, apprehension, and self-doubt. The very last thing I want to be visualizing in between the boxing ring ropes is my head rolling around on the canvas while strategizing how to avoid that fate. Isn't it obvious I want to be picturing and strategizing a stunning victory, the championship belt around my waist as I am hoisted onto the shoulders of adoring fans? I'll also need some pictures of the steps I'm going to take to achieve victory. I'll require an awareness of the incredible knockout punch I will unveil in order to make it onto the shoulders of my fans. That's a lot of pictures. But the image of my head rolling around the ring certainly doesn't need to be there.

On the other hand, there is advice based upon "always and never." One doesn't have to be a genius to figure out that in this life there is no "always" and there is no "never." There are certainly odds. There are absolutely personal preferences. And there are, without a doubt, behaviors and choices considered "the norm." Yes, there are strategies and approaches employed by numerous individuals that have led to success in the form of millions of dollars and/or worldwide fame. However, to be fair, we have to acknowledge that for every one of those individuals, there are many who chose the same strategy and went bust.

There is no always. Therefore, there is no never.

With this in mind, heed advice and rules which include these negative words, only when you add "badly" at the end.

Job interview sites tell us we should "Never get too personal on the job interview." Good advice? No. **Never get too personal...
badly**. In other words, if your personal story in conversation creates discomfort or reveals issues that will inhibit the interviewer from considering you for a job — you're doing it badly! On the other hand, if a personal story touches the interviewer's heart, and provides important insight into the kind of quality human being you are, chances are good you've not only found yourself a job, but you've made a friend for life. Who is to judge what's "too personal" anyway? Plus, as stated earlier, if you're in the job interview focusing on what you *shouldn't* do, how will any authentic or meaningful interaction ever take place? If your primary objective is to repress instincts that might make you go too far, becoming too personal and thereby breaking the "rule," how will the best of you ever see the light of day? Do you really think your most positive attributes are motivated by focusing on the worst-case scenario?

So, from this point forward let's apply the New Rule by taking all of those faulty pieces of advice and adding "badly" at the end. For example: actors in Hollywood are often cautioned: "Never drop off submissions (photos and resumes for casting consideration) in person."

No. **Never drop off submissions in person... badly**. The obvious intent of the advice is to spare you the acrimony that comes from annoying a professional who can open doors for you. (Submissions usually are preferred to come from a bona fide talent agent. The logic is, if every actor in town drove to the casting office to submit his or her materials, there would be an anxious crowd filling the casting office lobby, and no work would ever get done.) Avoiding the casting office removes the possibility of an actor being associated with this inconvenience. Good idea. What, though, if you drop off the submission really well, striking up a very brief and day-brightening interaction? What if the 10 seconds you spend in this person's presence forge a memorable and lasting impression that causes him or her to consider you for future opportunities? Well done! I suppose doing it badly means creating a nuisance that forges a memorable and lasting *negative* impression that causes the person to *not* consider you — so, don't do it badly.

A popular dating website says: "Don't talk too long on the phone initially. It could be fun, but it could also wear out your welcome. This is a really easy way to be misunderstood. Count this double when e-mailing."

What they really mean is: **don't talk too long on the phone... badly**.

Yes, if you are droning on long after your potential partner has lost interest...

THIS IS A BAD SIGN.

Isn't that simply a symptom of doing it badly? **Don't do it badly**.

I have heard many couples recount stories of talking on the phone for hours in their initial conversations because they instantly felt connected and comfortable with one another. They count it among their fondest memories, and point to it as the indicator that they had found "the one." Did they commit a dating crime? No. Because the rule is: **don't initially talk too long on the phone *badly*.**

But wait, there's more.

Never make a joke in a eulogy at a funeral? No. **Never make a joke in a eulogy at a funeral *badly*.** If your joke lightens the mood and helps the congregants more fondly remember the departed, it can be a healing and comforting gesture. Done badly... not so helpful... and extremely awkward.

Never keep your cell phone on during a public performance? No, just don't do it badly. If you are a doctor, and your phone has an unobtrusive vibrate mode, and you can receive a text that allows you to excuse yourself subtly while you return the call and save a life, that's not such a bad thing, is it? On the other hand, if you have *Macarena* as your ringtone on full blast, and there's no logical reason you should need to accept a call — turn the darn thing off! That's doing it *badly*. *Very badly.*

Don't flirt with the salesclerk in the bookstore where you purchased this book? No... you get the idea.

Often these "don't" rules are created for that express purpose: to keep us from doing things badly. Do we really need a rule to remind us we shouldn't annoy people, make them uncomfortable, or bore them with hours of monotonous conversation? Really?

Instead, let's agree to *always* do our best to... well... "do our best." That's the most that can ever be expected of us. And it allows us to act from a positive and passionate position rather than a fearful, protective one.

Now, what happens if you accidentally do it badly? What if the actor humbly and sensitively enters a casting director's office on just the wrong day at exactly the wrong time and is greeted with a torrent of expletive-filled venom? "How dare you come to my office hoping

to introduce yourself as a viable artist who might enhance my next
bleeping project?" "Take your bleeping friendly smile and impressive
promotional materials and shove—" uh, you know the rest. What do
you do now?

Have you made an enemy for life? Have you closed the door on
an opportunity that will end your career right here on the spot? "Why,"
you lament, "did I ever listen to that advice? Why didn't I just wait my
turn behind the thousands of other actors who are hoping for an
opportunity to contribute their talents to quality entertainment
industry projects? Now what am I going to do?"

Or, your face still stinging from the slap you received when you
invited the beautiful woman at the party to join you on the balcony
(unfortunately, badly), you ask yourself, "Why did I open my stupid
mouth? She knew she was beautiful. Why did she need me to tell her?
Now, do I duck out of the party and head to the neighborhood bar
for a bender of shame? What am I to do?"

Here's what you're going to do: apologize.

If you did it badly, or at an inopportune time, or in a way that
unintentionally caused harm (that would be doing it badly), you probably *are* sorry. Now is the time for a heartfelt and genuine apology.
Humble yourself. Let the person know your intent was only positive
and honorable, and you take responsibility for the "badly" in your approach. Place your 100% focus on making the person feel better, free
of excuses or justifications. Just apologize. If you need to send flowers
or drop off a steaming hot pizza, or offer to wash the person's car (!),
do it. Make amends.

Now, here's a hint that may be hard for some to accept. If the
executive is unable to accept your apology, and is vengeful and
punitive even after your heartfelt apologies and peace offerings...
he or she is now the one with the problem. If this is the case, there
is nothing for you to fix. Allow it. You'll never be able to change that
person because, as we've already established, you have zero power over

others, and your power begins with "I." Move on to the next opportunity. Chances are, with this person, some conflict would have arisen
regardless of your approach. There are few worse positions in life than
one in which we feel a need to reason with unreasonable people. The
more logic, authenticity, good intentions, and empathy we add to the
equation, the less reasonable they become. Move on, and try to do it
less badly next time. Learn from the results, but get back on the horse,
and continue taking action from a place of positive passion. Do your
best to not let this encounter reshape your New Rules of Thinking.

Did you catch that concept a couple sentences back, the idea of
"positive passion"? We're going to talk a lot more about that in a later
chapter. For the moment, though, it's important you understand this
idea of not doing things badly doesn't give you the freedom to do any
harmful or foolish thing you please. It gives you the freedom to do the
good things you please. Things that are positive; things about which you
are passionate and believe will have beneficial impact upon you and
the people around you.

(Hopefully, I don't need to clarify that we're talking about rules
here and not laws. You can't attach the word "badly" to the end of a
law as an excuse to break it. Example: don't drink and drive... badly...
doesn't work. Don't drink and drive *ever*. There is no good way to do it.
Laws are to be followed. No exceptions. Enough said?)

In a recent seminar I conducted for actors in Los Angeles, I
engaged a prominent film and television casting director in a conversation about the best way for hopeful actors to gain his attention. (If
you are unfamiliar with the Hollywood protocol, the casting director
is the professional who screens and chooses the many actors who will
have the opportunity to audition for a given role. Casting directors are
often, intentionally, very difficult to meet in person.) Very generously
and sincerely, my guest said, "Come to my office. If I have something right for you, I'll give you a shot." I was astounded. Here is a
high-powered casting executive actually inviting a group of 200 up-

and-coming actors to show up unannounced at his place of business to ask for an opportunity to read for a network television show (the project he was casting at the time).

Let me tell you what happened. First, as you might have guessed, only *three* out of the 200 worked up enough "courage" to visit the CD's office. I say "courage" because I can't help wondering how much nerve is required to show up to an office you were *invited* to visit. I mean, should he have sent a *limo to pick them up*? He said the words "COME TO MY OFFICE!"

It, painfully, reminds me of the time in the ninth grade when Sara Barjam looked me in the eyes and said, "Aren't you going to kiss me?" I didn't. Did I want to? Big time! Did she invite me to? Clearly. Well, what happened? Ahhh, some old rules and a lot of fear got in the way.

Back to the casting office. Of the three who managed to show up at his office, two were given auditions right on the spot, and I'm proud to say, one booked the job. Think of it, that's a career opportunity that would never have occurred had this actress followed the old rules or let fear govern her actions. And the hope is that her appearance on that program will lead to other opportunities that will be stepping-stones to the career of her dreams. The second actress was auditioned, but did not book the job (there can only be one person for the role). However, she gained a powerful interaction, and cemented her abilities in the consciousness of the casting director.

Win/win.

The third actress visited my studio a few days later and said to me, "I learned something. I'll never do that again. I went to this guy's office, and I saw him in the hallway. He brushed right past me as if I wasn't even there. It was awful." When I asked her what she did then, she replied, "I got the hell out of there." I sat her down and asked, "So, this is what you learned? Because he was too busy to welcome you with open arms, you will never go in-person to a casting office? Did he shout at you or in any way suggest you were unwelcome?"

"He ignored me!"

I gently explained to her that this was an example of seeking an opportunity "badly," which is breaking the New Rule. If you are so emotionally sensitive on your quest to make good things happen that you feel injured by the smallest events that don't match your expectations, your actions are not really serving the correct mission. *Your* actual goal was to feel good, to be welcomed, rather than *the* actual business goal of securing an opportunity. Instead of exclaiming, "Hey, Robert (or James or Michael), thanks for the invitation to come to your office! You were so informative at the seminar! I see you're busy. I'm going to pop in tomorrow," you took his non response as a "no."

Important distinction: A non response is not a "no."

After a lengthy chat, she resolved to do the logical thing: revisit the office, which she did. Not only did she get an audition on the second visit, she is a favorite at that casting office to this day.

As Benjamin Mee, the character Matt Damon plays in the movie *We Bought a Zoo*, so wisely advised his son, Dylan, "Sometimes all you need is 20 seconds of insane courage. Just literally 20 seconds of just embarrassing bravery — and I promise you... something great will come of it."

Be bold. Be confident. Do your best. If you do, you'll seldom break the rule of doing it badly.

Joint undertakings stand a better chance when they benefit both sides.

— Euripides

NEW RULE OF THINKING #2:

I Will Make The Choices That Make The Most Logical Business Sense

You're probably saying, "Duh."

I understand, but how often do we make a snap decision based on our *emotional* reaction before we have time to think about the logical impact of our decision? Many times, when faced with a difficult decision, the difficulty lies in the battle between what makes sense and what we want. Our emotions cloud our judgment, making us do and say things that do not contribute to the most equitable business conclusion. And when I say "business," I'm not only referring to work or career. In our relationships, we would do well to make the choices that would logically lead to the best and most lasting connection. Unfortunately, many times, what we *feel* in the moment is in conflict with those choices. Our insecurities, our fears, our self-centered needs rise up, causing us to make decisions that, frankly, do not make sense in the long run as part of the business of building, nurturing, and growing a relationship.

Suppose you're a department head in a mid-sized company. You have two employees who are candidates to fill a newly available supervisor position. Candidate A is a workhorse, always first to arrive at the office and last to leave. By far the most likable employee in the department, and a personal friend, Candidate A follows instructions to a "T," and is the one who will complete other employees' unfinished work.

Candidate B, a "neatnik," always has a spotless desk, works from a planning sheet daily, and therefore always finishes tasks in a timely fashion. Though Candidate B will not take on the tasks of other employees, he or she is always willing to share techniques that facilitate the completion of assigned tasks. Candidate B is not nearly as popular as Candidate A, mainly because he or she never hesitates to hold fellow employees accountable for completing delegated tasks.

Who is the choice to be your new supervisor? Which makes the most *business* sense?

Or… you are at a cocktail party where you strike up a conversation with a high-powered executive, far above your pay grade and station. The exec, right before leaving the party, hands you a business card, suggesting you keep in touch. Which is the best business choice:

A.   Don't call. You don't want to bother the exec. He or she will call you when the time is right.
B.   Call immediately — at midnight — when you get home.
C.   Call the next day, and thank the exec for an enjoyable conversation.
D.   Call every day.
E.   Keep the card, and wait for another encounter to justify making a call.

You probably noticed I refrained from telling you what I think the *right* answers are. This is where your business sense will need to kick in because each situation might have a different answer depending upon the circumstances. Remember, there is no *always* and there is no *never*. You do, however, have the ability to determine which is the best business choice, the most productive and positive choice that will bring about the best outcome.

It might help you to think of it this way: in every situation there is an *ultimate* goal that is greater, more rewarding, and more in line with who we really are than the short-term "instant-gratification" goal. If we can retain clarity as to what that actual long-range goal is, and create actions that move us toward it rather than farther away, this is the move that makes the most business sense.

Should you have a second piece of cake? Well, what is your ultimate goal? Have you set yourself on a course that demands a certain level of nutritional discipline? Or have you adopted a philosophy that says you can enjoy occasional extravagances as long as you put in extra time burning calories the next day? Or are you committed to simply enjoying and savoring life moment to moment, letting concerns of the flesh work themselves out on their own? Any one of these choices is your right to embrace; you'll just find it easier to determine the most logical business decision if you are absolutely clear what your actual objective is. If nutrition is your path, you can take great pleasure in moving a step closer to your goal by pushing away the second dessert. And if your goal is balance, you'll feel great both today with a mouthful of delicious cake, and tomorrow on the treadmill as you obliterate those calories. For those who live in the moment, bon appetit — and here's hoping every bite is savored to the fullest. In each situation, the most logical business decision can be made by giving thought to the ultimate goal, rather than struggling with the short-range dilemma.

My ultimate aim is to inspire others and to make the world a better place. That is the *business* of my life. Therefore, when someone has been rude to me, attempted to belittle me, or vented their anger in my direction, the most logical business decision is to master how "I" react to this perceived injustice, to practice patience and grace. Perhaps if I can get past my initial negative emotional responses (because in the long run, this person's anger or judgment has no meaningful impact upon my life when I embrace responsibility for my own happiness), I can even do something to brighten the day of "the perpetrator" or inspire them to be a little kinder to the next person they encounter. That serves my ultimate objective, and is therefore a smarter and more productive business decision.

Others would say to me they feel justified in standing up for themselves. To this I can only say: yes, stand up for yourself, but do it in a way that serves your ultimate goal, which probably is not to injure anyone who causes you discomfort. There is a way to hold your ground and assert your position without compromising your integrity.

It's not easy. In the moment, all sorts of emotions pop up threatening to cloud your judgment and your vision of your true business purpose in life. Be strong. Be visionary. When in doubt, step away from your personal involvement. Make the best business choice. That's the New Rule.

The truth of the matter is that you always know the right thing to do. The hard part is doing it.

— Norman Schwarzkopf

NEW RULE OF THINKING #3:
I Will Always Do The "Highest" Thing

Do the thing you feel in your heart is *right and just* for everyone involved. Yourself included. Do nothing you believe will bring harm to another being. Do the thing that will benefit the planet. Do the thing that is honest and true. It's different from *business* sense — it's *moral* sense. It's doing the right thing because you know it's right.

If your business is sales, approach your potential customers in a way you, yourself, would want to be approached. In relationships, do the thing that most honors the other person as a human being and someone who deserves respect. Deceive no one. Victories won by seizing upon the weakness or vulnerability of others will be hollow and will lead you to future difficulties. Do the highest possible thing you will feel good about when you go to sleep at the end of the day.

Does this mean you cannot be aggressive, resolute, even intractable in your methods? No. If you have determined your actions serve the greatest good for everyone, your passion will not only be required it can be appreciated and admired. Sometimes we have to be tough. But we can never be bullies. Sometimes our passion may lean to fanatical, but we can never lose sight of the greater good.

If you are ever in doubt as to what is the highest thing, seek counsel from someone whose integrity and goodness you admire. Perhaps they will offer a perspective to help you identify the highest thing.

At the end of the day, follow your heart, and do what is highest and most noble.

Most noble.

We tend not to use words like "noble" these days. But it's a good word. After all, if there is no nobility, no standard of honor in your actions and your philosophical approach, how can you expect the natural order of things to reward you? Certainly, on a daily basis you witness people enjoying prosperity who have little honor or ethics. But is that the world you want to create? Or would you rather generate your personal power to achieve the same results with integrity and generosity by doing the highest thing? You can. Simply ask yourself, "Is this the thing that is right and just for everyone involved? Is this a situation in which I'll be able to stand tomorrow and claim responsibility for the decision I made?" If it is, it is probably the highest thing.

Every so often when I pay for a purchase in cash at a convenience store or other venue, a clerk will accidentally give me change for a $20 instead of the appropriate change for the $10 bill I gave him or her. Let's say it's a gas station. It's really easy to think of huge oil companies that would never miss the extra 10 bucks and have certainly wrung huge amounts of money out of me for mere gallons of their precious and overpriced product. It would be tempting to pocket the $10 and later buy an extra… gallon and a half? But is it the highest thing? Is it the right thing for me? Is it the best thing for the clerk who will be responsible for the day-end tally? Is it the noble thing for the oil company?

Often when I visit an office building, I find myself holding the door for some harried person who charges through the doorway without a glance or any form of gratitude for the gesture. I am tempted to shout, "You're very welcome, your highness!" A clever comeback if I do say so myself. Is it the highest thing, though? Sure it will give me a moment of temporary satisfaction and alleged superiority. Maybe someone nearby will even roll their eyes as if to say, "Good one, buddy. That guy was a jerk." What, though, is the actual good? What has been accomplished that is useful, constructive or positive?

Nothing.

I have only succeeded at becoming the jerk myself; the judge and jury. I have no way of knowing that person's situation, or even if they whispered a "Thank you, you saved my life!" and I didn't hear it. Maybe the person wasn't a jerk at all. Furthermore, even if he was a jerk, why should I become a jerk, as well? Is that why I held the door, to exact gratitude from the passersby, doling out verbal punishment for all who dare to scramble by without rewarding my grand gesture with a shower of appropriate thanks? Is seizing the opportunity to make that person feel even a bit smaller really the highest thing I can do at this moment?

Probably not.

And if not, the New Rules say there's a better way to do it.

Do only the noble thing, the best thing, the right thing. You've heard the phrase "take the high road." Do it by choosing the most elevated action. Your reward may not be immediate, but it is coming... if you always do the highest thing.

*The real voyage of discovery exists
not in seeking new landscapes,
but in having new eyes.*

— Marcel Proust

NEW RULE OF THINKING #4:

I Will Make Every Effort To View All Challenges From A New Perspective By Seeing Them In A Different Way

By now, we've all heard the old saying, "The definition of insanity is repeating the same behavior and expecting a different result." We chuckle and nod our heads appreciatively. And yet, when it comes time to problem-solve on the job or in a relationship or in building a path to success, we often find ourselves doing exactly that: approaching the same problems with the same old solutions. We see that these solutions are ineffective, but we keep trying them again and again anyway. We rationalize there is only one solution, and sooner or later it *has* to work. After all, we've been told those are the rules; that's the way it's always been done, and the way it *should* be done.

And we drag out the other old saying, "If at first you don't succeed, try, try again."

However, the saying doesn't say try, try the *same tactics* again. If the first solution you choose doesn't work, doesn't it make sense to try another one? And another? And another, rather than buying into the idea that there is only one solution that needs to be repeated?

As a wide-eyed kid at my first blackjack table in Lake Tahoe, Nevada, it never occurred to me there were other solutions beyond "bet more," which I had recently been assured was the winning strategy by an "expert" on television. That solution didn't work on the first bet or the fifth or the fifteenth. Could it be the amount of the bet was not the real problem? Could I have looked at the game differently? Could I have seen my own participation in the game a different way, rather than applying the same solution over and over, hoping for a different result? Certainly, gambling and other games of chance depend highly on odds and other factors beyond our control. But the part of the process we *can* address is the way we see the game, and the strategies we apply. Now we can "try, try again" in perhaps a more effective manner with the hope of a new and better result.

This New Rule makes it clear there is never just one solution. All that is required is to see the problem from a different perspective, to see the things, people, and situations around you in a new way.

In my public speaking appearances, I often encounter groups that are very frustrated with certain elements of their lives. Their boss, for example, represents a huge immovable roadblock. Or their jobs themselves are filled with unwieldy difficulties. When I ask what is to be done about it, I am repeatedly told, "We have tried everything, but nothing seems to work."

Everything?

At this moment, I bring out a very common object, and I tell the crowd I have a huge dilemma: I can't, for the life of me, figure out what this thing is. It's a dilemma that requires a solution before we can continue the talk. I ask my audience to identify the object. Let's say it's a chair. Almost in unison, the crowd recites, "It's a chair." Problem solved!

"Are you sure?" I ask them. "Are you positive it can't be something else? Are you certain that 'chair' is the only answer?" After a moment of indecision, I step up onto the chair, and someone shouts out, "It's a stepladder!" Before I know it, people are volunteering 50 to 100 new possibilities of what this object might be, ranging from a coatrack to a weapon to a lion-taming device. Then, when we move to another subject, let's say a description of what this assemblage of people represents, the answers are many and varied. Finally when I raise the question of the immovable obstacle previously discussed, the participants are able to see that boss or problematic issue or relationship in a completely new manner. As we move to possible solutions, suddenly the options seem plentiful. All because the group gave themselves permission to see things in a new light. They initiated a fundamental re-training of their problem-solving process, and discovered they have many more available options than they had ever thought possible.

You should experiment with this concept. Look around where you are right now. Choose an object that has previously only held one identity for you. A cup? A book? Now, take a moment to find 10 other things that object might actually be. Don't hold back, and don't be afraid to get creative. Have fun with it.

Once you have completed that exercise, think of something that has posed a problem for you, something for which you have yet to find a suitable solution. Try the same exercise. Push yourself to conceive 10 alternative solutions. Again, don't limit yourself — be as creative as you wish. Now see if any of those solutions are viable. Whether they are or not, you've proven to yourself that there is always more than one answer, no matter how insurmountable the obstacle may seem.

Granted, solutions to difficult issues are not always available at the drop of a hat, but choosing to view things from a different perspective helps our creative juices flow, reducing the frustration as we attempt to find new answers, and allowing us to approach the situation from a positive place rather than from a negative one.

Try at this moment to think of it not as a new idea but as a New Rule. A new way you will approach your problems. And because it's a rule, like the carpenter's hammer, you will use it as a constant tool in your problem-solving activities. See the problem from a new perspective. Look at it in a different way. Find new and more creative answers. Then and only then is it time for you to shape a strategy as to how you will solve the problem. If you jump in trying to solve an issue before you've taken the time to look at it from new and varied perspectives, you always approach it with the same tactics, and probably achieve similar inferior results. And if you're looking for different results, better results, more spectacular results, it would stand to reason that you would want to use your New Rule to find a new approach, a new solution, a new technique, and possibly a new attitude to bring you the fresh results you desire.

If you find you are having trouble seeing new possibilities and new perspectives, sometimes it really helps to enlist the input of someone you trust. Someone who can shake things up a bit and allow you to see the situation from a different angle. Who is that person in your life? Someone creative, open-minded, and someone whose opinions you value? It has to be someone who won't limit your possibilities, won't ridicule your new approach, and won't spout the old rules telling you there's only one solution. If you have such a person in your life, call on them. You will be glad you did. If you can't think of a person you know, the libraries and the internet are filled with the words of great creative thinkers who perhaps might give you a fresh perspective to help you find a powerful new solution to your "same old" problem.

There is only one age-old, inevitable Grim Reaper dilemma to which we have not yet been able to find or create a solution. We all know what that is. Nobody gets out alive. Modern medicine and science are working hard to solve that one, too. For everything else, there is always a new solution if only you are willing to look at each dilemma from a different perspective, giving yourself the ability to see it in a unique way and solve it in a brand-new and more effective manner.

Try it, you'll like it.

Do not look backward in anger, or forward in fear but around in awareness.

— James Thurber

NEW RULE OF THINKING #5:

I Will Make Decisions Based Upon What I Love Rather Than What I Fear

Psychologists will tell you there are only two options in every action we take. **Love** and **fear**. These are the unseen governing forces determining each of our physical outcomes. You either act from love or from fear.

Some would say this is simply a question of semantics. If it is, so be it. Let's follow it anyway. When we make decisions attempting to prevent or mitigate something negative or something we fear, our entire approach is at odds with the very nature of who we are. And usually, in this state, we are far less effective, dynamic, empathetic, and much less happy than when we act from love.

The semantics of it would be, if you insist your children carry sweaters because they might catch cold, that is a fear-based instruction. If you make the same decree, this time because you want them to be warm and toasty so they can enjoy the evening out, it places you and the children in an entirely different frame of mind. As you become more aware of choosing the positive state on a regular basis, you will see that the people around you respond in a much more positive and meaningful way. Is it magic? No, it is a shift away from a less-effective field of energy than you might normally use.

If you arrive early every day to work because you fear that if you are late you will lose your job, it places you in an entirely different mindset than when you take the same measures because you want to give yourself time to prepare for a great start of the day. Semantics? Maybe. Effective? Yes.

The objective here is to constantly occupy your mind with what you *want*, not what you *don't want* (sound familiar?). You want to place all of your energy into the things you would have happen in your life rather than allowing your fear to direct your own energy to attract the things you hope will not happen. Our time on this planet is limited. That is a certainty. Why then would we spend even one of those precious minutes pondering the elements we seek to avoid when we can achieve the same result by choosing a real and positive goal instead? We can take the action of saying, "Don't go out without a sweater! You'll catch your death of cold!" Or we might instead try, "You'll enjoy the football game more if you're warm and toasty! Take a sweater!" The child's sweater gets worn either way — so why fill his or her mind with the possibility of illness? The "Thanks, Mom" or "Thanks, Dad" you might receive when you pose the solution from a loving place will feel a lot better to both you and your child.

Rushing to your place of employment with morbid thoughts of reprimands, unemployment, and abject poverty will not contribute to the most productive day. Why stress yourself on the way to work when you can fill the trip with excitement and unlimited possibility?

You are in charge of your perspective; no one else is. You have the power to choose the platform from which you operate. If you choose the protective, combative, and stressful position of fear, the success you seek will not only seem further away, but you might have less ability to enjoy it if and when it does finally arrive.

Think about what you love, and see the things around you from a place of possibility. Allow your feelings to resonate with excitement and hope as you make your decisions. Don't wait for permission to act from love. It is always your choice. And if you think about it, common sense tells us there should be no other way to think.

Is it possible bad things may still happen in your life? Not only possible — certain. Won't it be difficult enough to deal with those things when they actually do happen without suffering the regret of having squandered the time that should have been joyous and hopeful worrying about the bad that might occur? So don't despair or lose your belief in yourself when tough times arrive.

It is said that worry is just a prayer for what you *don't* want to happen. Now, I'm not insisting you believe in prayer from a religious point of view. I'm simply saying what you occupy your thoughts with eventually becomes your reality. Don't you often find yourself saying, "I *knew* that was going to happen!" Well, of *course* you did! It was what you focused upon all day.

Some of my clients have shared with me the concept that they tend to approach things from the negative because they don't want to get their hopes up. They figure if they go into every situation expecting the worst, they won't suffer the crushing disappointment that sometimes sets them back with a week or so of depression and recovery when that worst thing happens. They don't want to get their expectations too high, so instead they shift their focus to the things that could go wrong, and if things work out they'll be pleasantly surprised. In doing this, they unknowingly make the possible problems and the worry that comes with those problems their primary focus. And history has shown that what we focus on becomes what is. Therefore, lowered expectation almost guarantees us a lesser result — created by our own power!

The idea of not wanting to get your hopes up is very understandable. Disappointment can be very hard to manage. Here is a valuable piece of advice:

Instead of lowering your expectation, get better at dealing with disappointment.

Yes, work at it. Become more effective at recovering from the hopes that don't pan out, and quicker to replace those thoughts with more creative and effective strategies to achieve success the next time around. (If you need help, remember the New Rule that reminds you to see things from a new perspective.) It just makes more sense.

A person who is not the greatest swimmer certainly has the right to harbor concerns about drowning. But rather than occupy his or her mind with fearful visions of drowning, rather than avoiding the water altogether or giving way to panic, wouldn't it be more productive to fill the mind with thoughts of how to become a better swimmer by taking a class he or she might love, or learning what is necessary to become his/her own lifeguard (how about a life preserver)? Much more preferable to spending every moment at the water's edge worrying about what bad things might happen. Or if one chooses not to swim, wouldn't the day be better spent devising strategies to enjoy the scenery, the company of others and more, whether you venture into the water or not? What good does the worry do you?

How many relationships have you witnessed where one partner resents the other participating in activities with friends or co-workers, like going out for cocktails or dancing, or even taking a class or seminar, because down deep they are *afraid* their loved one will meet or flirt with (or worse) someone new at the bar, club, or school? Isn't the loving action to focus on your trust in your partner while encouraging them to do the things they find fun or educational? Instead, many people prevent these pleasant experiences simply because their worry (fear) that they will lose something is stronger than their natural instinct to show love.

Driving to the dentist's office, if you give way to fear and find yourself thinking how horrible the procedure is going to be and how much it will hurt, that will be your only impression of the appointment. If, instead, you concentrate on the improvement of your dental health, how much brighter your smile will be, and the artistry of your dentist, you may find that the painful parts seem less profound.

When your fear of rejection causes you to occupy your thoughts with what a disaster the relationship with your mother-in-law has become, it causes you to act from a defensive and sometimes judgmental position, which, in turn, manifests even more of the strain in the relationship. Why not review the positive aspects of the woman who, if nothing else, gave birth to someone you love? Why not focus on one positive moment you will spend together, with the hope that this one moment can become two, and so on?

You must remember, most of the time these negative choices are inspired by fear.

It is true that fear can be a useful and necessary tool. It reminds us of precautions we need to take; it forces us to organize our thoughts and remind ourselves to stay on track and act in responsible ways; it pushes us to keep alert and ready to handle adverse situations. However, once these reminders have been registered, if fear becomes the motivating sponsor of our actions, the actions we take will surely lead us to the very place we were attempting to avoid. Now let's talk about fear a little more.

It's always easy to tell someone not to be afraid, but for the one experiencing the fear, mere words are usually hugely insufficient to improve the situation. Many times we find ourselves in a state of fear simply because we assume that's where we should be. We base this upon past history, what we see in the media, and the rumblings of other people.

At a recent dinner party, there was a sudden power outage and the guests and hosts were all thrown into pitch-black darkness. One of the guests let out a scream and began spiraling into a state of panic. When asked if she was afraid of the dark, she replied that she was not, but "the power went out!" In other words, this guest had no actual fear of the dark, but had convinced herself hysteria in a blackout was appropriate and necessary. Thus the screaming and panic. Of course this racket proved very unsettling to the other guests, raising the level of anxiety much higher. Even after one of the hosts eventually secured a candle and a match, bathing the room in a somewhat romantic glow, the anxious atmosphere continued.

Why? Because there was a real consequence? Was there some imminent danger? In truth, there was panic and anxiety simply because it seemed like there should be.

And what does this fear accomplish other than to render us less effective in dealing with the situation at hand? The candle and matches might have been located minutes sooner had there been less focus on calming the panic in the room. The flicker of the candle might have sparked a lovely conversation about past romantic dinners. Fear, however, often tends to be a first reaction, almost a reflex, a knee-jerk response that renders us far less capable of handling the events in front of us, far less powerful and dynamic. And why would we ever choose to be in that state if we could avoid it?

My acting students constantly report to me their performance was diminished because they were experiencing fear. I ask them what they were afraid of and most times the question cannot be answered. "What did you fear was going to happen?" I ask.

"I was afraid I'd mess it up."

"And then what would happen?"

"I don't know. Nothing, I guess."

"Were you afraid we might laugh at you or think less of you?"

"Not really."

Now, in other conversations, the person has responded with a passionate, "Yes!" They were petrified the room would be filled with laughter, and they would be perceived as a failure. Here, I have to take them back to the earlier point that while there is always the possibility of failure, to worry about it and fill our thoughts with echoes of the negative result we want to avoid only serves to compromise our actions, ensuring a less positive result. How about, I ask them, concentrating on the good you might do, the information you might deliver, and, if nothing else, the hearty and refreshing laugh you might give your audience?

But, back to the conversation in question:

"Was there," I continue, "any threat of physical or emotional harm?"

"No."

"Then why did you choose fear?"

And the real answer most of the time is the same:

Habit.

We are in the habit of choosing fear rather than love. Keep in mind these actors are doing the thing they love most to do in all the world in my classroom, what many of them were born to do. Yet they choose fear.

I work with corporate team members who love what they do, believe wholeheartedly in their products and services, and have absolutely no doubt the information they can share about their company is of immeasurable value. But when it comes time to stand before a group of associates with a presentation, or to negotiate with a headstrong client, or confront an underachieving subordinate or an irate customer, these capable businesspeople choose fear.

Couples I meet want nothing more in life than to share their days with someone with whom they can be open, vulnerable, playful, and affectionate. Yet, in the moments of truth, they shut down, storing up regrets of the things they wish they had said and done.

Why? Fear.

Skeptics would suggest this fear is not a choice. I would contend we have the power to control our own lives and therefore our fears, and that the state from which we operate is indeed a choice. It takes conditioning and work, but it is possible, and it is absolutely necessary.

The real point here is we often waste a lot of precious time and energy and we suffer a great deal of unnecessary anxiety before we really even know what it is we fear. There are a great many real things in this world of which to be afraid. The last thing we want to do is place ourselves in a state of fear simply out of habit. This is why I'm asking you to identify the things or the consequences you fear. If there really is no consequence, skip over the fear.

Don't choose fear — use fear.

Rather than opt for fear out of habit, because you simply assume it's time to panic, *use* fear as a guide, a coach, a motivator, a reminder of areas you need to focus and modify. Then you can move on to the powerful, positive actions you can employ to make the most of the situation.

Also remember that some of the symptoms you may be interpreting as fear are really signs of excitement. Maybe you've no need to be afraid at all. You simply misinterpreted your excitement as the onset of fear. And, of course, once your brain tells your body "we're in fear mode," the body takes on a life of its own. What would happen if you stopped to examine the possible consequences, the worst-case scenario? The absolute worst case... and you found it was nothing you couldn't handle?

- The presentation doesn't go well; the audience laughs at your speech.
- The headstrong client storms out of the room.
- The irate customer becomes... even more irate.

What if then you chose to approach the task at hand from a place of love rather than fear? Imagine how much more capability would be at your disposal. Imagine how much more enjoyable the experience would be.

If, on the other hand, you discover there is truly some impending danger of which you should be afraid...

- The rattlesnake *is* actually under the bed. Should I grab it?
- I am tipsy and need to get home. Should I drive?
- Should I transfer 80% of my life savings to this pyramid concept?

- The drunken brawler in the bar has challenged me to a fight. What to do?

...well, this would be a good time to evaluate your course of action, making a loving (and safe) choice that places you at your most effective when you really need it. Fear can be a valuable tool in protecting you in times of danger, though it cannot and must not become a default.

Some would say regarding the first example above, "Well, maybe for you, a well-known public speaker, an audience laughing at you is not a big deal, but for me it's the worst thing imaginable." I empathize with this, and yet I have to point out that if the audience reaction is the most important thing to you, it suggests you were not specific as to your true intent. In other words, it seems being loved/appreciated/applauded by the audience was a higher priority than the delivery of valuable information, enlightenment, or entertainment. That would take you back to the New Rule that guides us to choose actions based upon what best serves our true business intent. When you generously choose to share your knowledge or talent with a group of people, your objective remains the same, whether they respond by throwing rose petals or tomatoes. When I give a motivational speech, it's not about me. It's about the people I hope to motivate. And it is their prerogative to respond any way they see fit. Of course, I hope they will respond with cheers and adulation, but their response is beyond my control and, therefore, nothing I should fear. Instead, I should focus on what I can control: my delivery of the speech without the obligation to insert fear into the equation.

If they choose to laugh at me, I can choose to laugh along because there really is no consequence either way.

If there is no consequence, reject fear.

Choose love.

Why not occupy your consciousness with the things you love?

It works.

*There's only one corner of the universe
you can be certain of improving,
and that's your own self.*

— Aldous Huxley

"I" VS. "ME":

The Pronoun Challenge

Okay, let's pause a moment to continue with the new language to go with our New Rules. If we've established that "I" is the best and highest part of us, we also have to talk about "Me." "Me" is the part of us that gets in the way, the part that believes the old rules, and subscribes to the idea that other people and events control our destiny. "What about me?" "Look what you did to me!" "How will this affect me?" "What are people thinking about me?"

"Me" is the one looking for someone to blame, some obstacle that cannot be overcome, some reason why fear is an appropriate first choice. "Me" is the voice in your head that speaks to you unkindly and rationalizes reasons why you should not attempt the efforts that might bring you joy and success. "Me" says, "What if I fail?" Or, "This isn't really what I want." It's the voice that tells you you're too busy, too tired, or too sick to pursue the dream that means so much to you. And most of the time "Me" *sounds* like the voice of reason, offering prudent advice such as, "Someday, but not today. It's just not the right time."

If you want to change, if you want your life to be fully realized and filled with reward and bounty, and you find it isn't, the problem is "Me."

Here's a perhaps silly yet interesting exercise: Just for fun, take a few seconds and say the word "Me" a few times.

Really. Try it.

Look what "me" does to your face; your tone, even your mood. Not pretty, is it? Very nasal, almost whiny. It even makes some people scrunch up their faces in a way that isn't particularly complimentary.

Now try saying "I" a few times.

"I."

Nice, huh? Smooth, relaxing, almost as if it's coming from deep inside you. If you will, allow that feeling to remind you to think of "me" as the less-desirable version of you, and "I" as the all-powerful one, with whom all possibilities begin.

Now, you're going to have to work with me here. You're going to need to take a leap of faith because what I'm about to suggest might be very difficult to embrace. It may fly in the face of most everything you hold to be true… because most everything you hold to be true, and everything I hold to be true, and everything anyone holds to be true, is also, like this very life we're living, an illusion. Yes, I said it: our beliefs are *illusions*. A minute is a minute only because a consensus of people have told you it's a minute. You point to your front lawn and say the color is green only because so many people have told you that's what it is. Yet each of us has no way of knowing whether others are registering the same color we're seeing in our own heads. We simply agree it's green. Every truth and value each of us holds dear is simply the illusion we have chosen to embrace. And that's not a bad thing. We all have to believe in something. But when we hold those beliefs as *absolute* truths, as incontrovertible facts, those beliefs can become limitations, robbing us of our power to control our destiny and improve our lives.

Easy now. I'm not challenging your beliefs or attempting in any way to tell you what is right or wrong. I'm only telling you that from the moment you're born you make choices about what is true, what is right, what is wrong, what is beautiful, what is desirable and more. In some societies, sitting on the floor is common and acceptable, others not so much. Someone decided it's okay if I kiss you on the cheek, yet on the lips is forbidden. And that's okay if we all agree, and it fits within our plan to make the most of this life. But if that belief is limiting, like in some societies where a woman has fewer rights or less power, where a person of color is not considered equal, where a child earns less respect than an adult but is valued more than a senior citizen, and that belief becomes a wall preventing you from moving in the direction you most want to go, then your beliefs become a hindrance to your growth and success.

Let's keep it straight, the problem is not our beliefs. The problem is that "Me" part of us that uses those beliefs to limit our possibilities. It's only a problem when what we believe robs us of our power to create more abundance of the things that make us truly happy.

So the starting point in any positive change is making a change in what you believe about you. What you can do, who you can be, and what is possible.

If you're convinced the problem is your boss, or the problem is your husband or your wife, or the problem is your income or your weight or the mistakes your parents made, do yourself the biggest favor ever: let them off the hook and shift the focus to yourself because the problem is never the adversity; it's how we react to the adversity. Someone once said it's not a question of altitude, how high you climb, but of attitude, how you perceive the journey. Are you happy right now? If not, what's the problem? I mean in this very moment, what's stopping you from experiencing happiness? Sure there is a collection of memories from the past that have contributed to your mood, but right this very moment there is only this moment and it's your choice how you feel at this specific point in time.

I know, sometimes it feels like the universe is working against us. It feels like everyone else is winning except us. That's simply the illusion, the dream. And remember, you're the director of your part of the dream. Whatever you believe, that's what is. Are you beautiful? It depends upon what you believe. Are you wealthy? What is wealth to you? Have you achieved success? Well, what is your personal measure of success? More importantly, what do you believe are the obstacles standing in the way of your success? If you believe those obstacles are external — people, rules, history, the opinions about us, prejudices, and innuendo — then you have lost your power to create change because we all know you can't change others. You can't fight City Hall. In truth, you can inspire change, although it's often a long and slow process and it still begins with the alterations you make in your personal belief system because the universe is not working against you. It is working for you. And those others who are beyond your control are not the problem. Nor is City Hall. Any problem we have with our experience of this incredible world is the product of "Me."

As a result, if the problem is "Me," that's the best news in the world because "Me" is the one thing you do have the power to change, the right to change. And it's simply a process of letting go of our own self-righteous absolute truth — the idea that the things we believe are the only truth — and understanding that those beliefs provide insurmountable obstacles and limits beyond which we cannot climb. Once we understand there are no limits because our experience is whatever we shape it to be, we are free to create the life of our choice.

Your boss is a jerk? That's his or her prerogative. Not your problem until how you react to it makes it your problem. Suppose you thought less about how his or her behavior affects "Me," granted your boss the right to be a jerk, and continued to do your work without expectation, without needs, without judgment. It wouldn't change your boss, but it would certainly change your reaction to your boss... which would then change your actions. Once your actions changed, chances are, your results would change. As you achieve more positive results, it's just possible your boss might make choices other than being a jerk, which then might encourage others around you to make better efforts with better actions and better results. Pretty soon the positive spiral begins, and all because you made a change, not a change in your boss (that's not within your power), but a change in you. Actually... a change in "I."

If you're thinking, "I knew that"... you did. The problem often is, even as we acknowledge the truth of it, we do nothing about it. We succumb to the thinking we are victims, we are small and powerless. And the reality is, if our intention is to change the people, places, and things around us, we probably *are* quite small. Yet when we understand that this dream is shaped by how we change ourselves, our thoughts, our reactions to the people and events around us, we soon discover we are all-powerful.

One deep breath at this very moment: one powerful decision to choose gratitude for this moment, one action designed to move "I" closer to the prosperity we most desire, changes the "now" and every moment that follows. Will it change your bank account? Not at this moment. Not by magic. There is no leprechaun who will guide you to a pot of gold. But in this moment, in this "now," there will be peace, and joy, and all possibility. And if now is filled with promise, it stands to reason the next moment will be better than expected a moment ago, and so on, and so on. And as each moment becomes filled with more possibility, slowly or perhaps quickly we begin to realize that a winning lottery ticket is not really what we wanted or needed in the first place. We only *thought* what we are all actually searching for — peace of mind, joy, and hope — would be gained through the lottery ticket. And we all know how it goes with that.

If we can get "Me" under control, and place our focus upon, and our trust in, "I," we find ourselves much closer to the "knowing" that leads to fulfillment and unlimited potential.

Right where we belong.

You, as much as anybody in the entire universe, deserve your love and affection.

— Buddha

NEW RULE OF THINKING #6:
I Will Fire The Announcer

If you're anything like me, you have a voice in your head, talking nonstop, 24/7. In my case, one of my greatest difficulties late at night is turning the voice off so I can get some sleep. The voice won't shut up. It wants to keep on working, keep coming up with ideas, keep reviewing the day's events. It also keeps flashing me little meaningless snippets of sound and visual bites from the day, and the day before, and the day before that. Then, right in the middle of recapping the business meeting that took place during the day, Scooby Doo appears and says "Ranks, Reorge!" Next, a snippet of an old song, and suddenly back to the meeting. And throughout the whole thing, a voice is narrating the action.

For a lot of you, that voice is going full steam right now. And what good is it doing you? Is it making the moment any better? Probably not. In fact, it's probably just getting in the way of you absorbing and understanding what I'm trying to tell you. Some of you can hardly process these words right now because the voice in your head is saying: "You know what? He's absolutely right. I never thought of it that way. I do have a voice in my head. There it is! Hello, hello, hello, hello.... testing... one, two, three. There it is again! Ooh! Somewhere... over the rainbow."

And by now you've missed the whole point of what I'm saying.

And I know what you're thinking. "But that's me talking. I have to listen." Well, I've got some news for you.

That voice isn't you. *You*... or as we've been saying, *"I"*... is not the voice. *"I"*... is the person who is listening to the voice. The observer. The one experiencing the voice. The one feeling whatever those words make you feel. The voice is just the announcer. Is it necessary? Mostly... no. It's like when you watch a baseball game on television. *You*... are watching the game... experiencing the game... hopefully enjoying the game. The baseball announcer is mostly telling you things you already knew, "And... the windup... the pitch... a swing and a miss!" No kidding. You knew that. You just watched it happen. Did you really need some guy who is farther away from the action than the view you have through the television cameras to tell you the batter swung and missed? Ninety percent of the stuff this announcer is telling you is simply that... commentary on the obvious.

The voice in your head is pretty much the same:

"Wow, it's hot in here!" Yeah, tell me something I didn't already know.

"Hey, this woman next to me is totally hot!" Duh. Thanks a lot, Captain Obvious. But, the plot thickens. Because the voice... the announcer also has a tendency to add in commentary that messes things up, things that simply aren't true, or are mere speculation. It starts to say, "Not only is she hot, she's also totally ignoring me. In fact, she hates my guts! She thinks she's too good for me. Why do women hate me so much? Why did I even come here in the first place? My life totally sucks. Well, who needs you, Miss Too Good For Anybody?"

Meanwhile, at the very same time, the announcer in the woman's head might be reporting: "Hey, this guy next to me keeps looking at me. Hmmm. Very attractive. But he keeps glancing over here and saying nothing. He must have seen me playing that stupid game on my cell phone. And now he's frowning. He probably thinks I'm some low-class person who has no right to be here. Who is he to judge me? Well, who needs you, Mr. Thinks He's All That!"

You get the idea.

And you assume all of this chatter is true, and it is meaningful information because it's *you* talking to *you*. And haven't we all been taught to listen carefully to our thoughts — that little voice in our heads — to avoid being impulsive by thinking things out? Isn't it our responsibility to listen to the "announcer" to be true to ourselves?

The announcer is not you. The announcer is just a voice in your head. If you want to achieve more, experience more, accomplish more...

Fire the Announcer.

Yes, fire the announcer. Why? Because pretty much everything the announcer is telling you is stuff you already knew. And most of the other stuff the announcer adds is meaningless improvisation.

Fire the announcer.

Hire the coach.

Who is the coach?

Think of the coach as the entity that simply tells you to get to work enjoying, digesting, and taking action on what you're experiencing. Even at the baseball game, *sometimes* the announcer serves a great purpose: filling you in on facts you didn't know, statistics, colorful background, and directing your attention to things you might not have noticed. Keeping your head in the game.

Like a coach.

Most often, that voice is just providing commentary. You may have decided long ago that the voice is the one who keeps you safe; who helps you process the moments of your life. In actuality, the voice is just getting in your way, talking you into things that aren't helpful, talking you out of things that would be productive, and distracting you from the best parts of the experience.

You want success? You want joy? You want fulfillment?

Fire the announcer.

Don't trust the voice. What does it know anyway? Do we really think there is some wisdom that we need the announcer to share that our hearts haven't already figured out? Our hearts.

There is a wonderful scene in the movie *City of Angels* in which Seth, a compassionate angel of death, played by Nicolas Cage, falls in love with a mortal surgeon, played by Meg Ryan. She, of course, has difficulty believing he is who and what he says he is. His existence flies in the face of every part of her training, everything she has come to believe as a student of medical science. How, she wonders, can she believe in "angels," in something she cannot see with her own eyes?

Seth asks her to close her eyes and extend her hand, which she does. He runs his finger across the palm of her hand, and while her eyes are still closed, he asks her if she knows what he is doing.

"You're touching me."

"How do you know, if you can't see it?" he asks.

"Because I *felt* it."

Seeing is not believing. It is not necessarily true that when you see it you can believe it. It may be more true that when you believe it, you will see it.

Most of the doubts, fears, and hesitations in the crucial moments of your life were simply suggestions from the announcer. You suspected they weren't valid or necessary because of what you felt, but perhaps you listened anyway and were led further away from the fulfillment you deserve.

It gets worse.

Because you have come to believe the voice is you, you have a tendency to maintain a very personal relationship with this voice, which encourages the announcer to speak to you just about any way it pleases. The New Rules are designed to strengthen "I" and the way you see yourself, as well as your appreciation of the world in which you live. Sometimes that voice in your head gets out of control, speaking to you in ways you would never speak to other people or allow them to speak to you. Sometimes it's downright abusive. And it's bad enough someone is speaking to you this way, eroding your confidence, demeaning your character, but it's nothing short of a crime when the perpetrator is *you*.

And it has a very detrimental effect. Any influence that subliminally lowers your opinion of "I" is harmful. Imagine if you were training for a marathon, a grueling 26.2-mile endurance contest so demanding that the mere act of finishing, regardless of the time, is worthy of celebration. Now imagine, as you train for this ordeal, that your trainer, a person you trust, a person whose opinion means the world to you, is running alongside you every step of the way shouting, "You suck! You're a loser! You'll never finish, why even bother? What is a fat pig like you even thinking running a race like this?" Imagine the harmful effect over time.

Well, this is what we do to ourselves when we allow the voice in our heads to undermine us. It's subtle, yet extremely damaging, the same way even the tallest mountain can be eroded over time by drops of rain. Seems minor at the time, but gradually the impact is devastating.

One of the most important tenets of your quest for success is belief in your own integrity. How could you possibly feel a sense of integrity in someone who speaks to you in the lowest and crudest manner? And in reverse, when you hear these slurs hour after hour, year after year, how can you help but begin, in the deepest recesses of your consciousness, to believe these atrocious statements are true?

Stop it.

That's what you MUST say to the voice in your head: "Stop it! Speak respectfully to me. It is certainly your prerogative, Voice, to correct me, critique me, guide me, even chastise me for my errors. But, I demand that you do it in a respectful manner. And it wouldn't be the worst thing in the world if you were nurturing, encouraging, and supportive." That's really not too much to ask, although for now, the New Rules simply require that you refuse to be your own detractor.

There are enough people in the world who would, unintentionally or otherwise, rip at the seams of your self-image. We hear a lot in the news about efforts to stop bullying in schools. Well, bullying doesn't only happen to children. It happens in the workplace and in shopping malls and certainly in traffic, both perpetrated and absorbed by people of all ages, and the pain and damage is just as real as it is for a child. Often, these bullies don't realize what they are doing. Perhaps they think that's just their way of communicating forcefully or engaging in humor, or they are subconsciously making themselves feel better. Whatever the reason for this behavior, it's not healthy for you, and the New Rules prohibit it. When it comes to others, it's your choice how to deal with them. Remember, we cannot control others. Our happiness is generated by the changes we make in ourselves. Therefore, it's not always necessary to confront or educate the bullies in our lives. "I" can choose to ignore the bullying of others by focusing on what "I" know to be my personal truth. "I" can also generously "gift" that person the freedom to be the bully he has chosen to be, understanding that his point of view does not control my behavior, my emotions, or my power to achieve success. That person is just another "announcer" — probably working for the opposing team, with his or her own set of meaningless and often erroneous observations. He is not the game. Only a biased observer. So, why would I waste any time arguing with the visiting team's announcer when the game is raging on before my very eyes? I wouldn't, if I really want to win the game! Imagine a football quarterback charging off the field in the middle of a play to confront and correct the people in the broadcast booth! He or she wouldn't do it; nor should we. The only thing more laughable would be a scenario in which that same player races to exchange insults with his or her *own* team's commentators! Or is it laughable?

Any responsible team owner would do the reasonable thing: fire the announcer!

There are enough distractions in the game of life without introducing more from within the home organization. You'll withstand enough insults, speculation, and denigration from others — the opposing crowd, the other team, and so on. You cannot afford to have your own inner voice join the "pecking party." The voice in your head can and must be one of your most trusted advisors. That voice must represent clarity, good counsel, and authenticity. The voice of reason. A friend. That voice must be a good *coach*.

You must also do your best to keep your word to yourself. I know that's a tough one. We constantly make small promises to ourselves that we cannot keep. Think of the countless New Year's resolutions: the additional pieces of pizza we swore we wouldn't eat, the household projects, the money we would responsibly save, the list goes on. And many times we mean to keep these promises, we really do, but... things happen. Well, every time we fail to come through on one of those promises, the integrity of our personal image suffers. Especially when it's a promise we never intended to keep in the first place.

It may sound like a cliché but be authentic to yourself. Be respectful. Show personal integrity to the person who matters most. "I." And if this announcer in your head cannot step up and become a coach, a mentor, a supporter... fire him... fire her. If that voice is constantly stating the obvious, casting judgments, putting you down, inserting statements that are untrue and harmful to your self-esteem, that voice is not a coach. You will learn to differentiate the coach from the announcer because the coach is giving you encouragement, calling your attention to elements you may not have noticed, keeping you focused on the best parts of your game. The announcer is just talking because he or she has a microphone.

You'll have to work at it. It will take patience and effort to separate the useless and often untrue commentary from the valuable coaching that goes on in your head. Still, you can do it. Just practice observing your thoughts before you react to them. Ask yourself which thoughts are simply obvious play-by-play, and which are important instruction and reminders. Many people tell me that a few daily minutes of meditation can be a great help. Take the opportunity a few times a day to clear your mind of all thoughts, simply listening to your own breathing. As phrases come into your mind, just observe them as you would a movie at the local cineplex. Let them pass through unexplored, and return to the sound of each breath. After you have done this for a reasonable period, it will be easier to separate the sound of the announcer from the words of the coach. Your heart will tell you when something is valuable enough for you to make an investment of your time, energy, and emotions. In time it will also become painfully obvious which thoughts are laughably irrelevant. Those thoughts are the announcer.

Fire the announcer and trust your heart.

Because you feel it.

*One person with a belief is equal to the force
of ninety-nine who have only interests.*

— John Stuart Mill

NEW RULE OF THINKING #7:

If I Can Fix A Situation, I'll Get To Work; If I Cannot, I Will Allow It And Release It

There are some things we cannot control. That's a maddening thought for those of us who strive to always be in control, but as the musician Bruce Hornsby sang, "That's just the way it is."

We squander precious time and energy fighting against the things we cannot control. If we acknowledge there are certain "givens" over which we have no control, and simply allow these factors to exist while we direct our energies to what we can control, we find ourselves in a far better place.

There are many things that, while their presence is not our first choice, we can certainly endure the fact that they exist. How did the singer Frank Sinatra phrase it? "That's life!"

A while back I had the opportunity to purchase an interest in a condominium in Palm Springs, California, which my family now uses as a getaway vacation spot. Now, Palm Springs in the summer can reach temperatures of up to 120 degrees. What sense would it make to constantly run around complaining about the heat? That's just, says Mr. Hornsby, the way it is! And once I simply allow that it gets very hot, I cease to object to it. I certainly notice it, but I allow it. It is out of my control. What I can control is where I go in Palm Springs... the pool, many air-conditioned restaurants, movie theaters, water parks, etc. I can control *when* I go... the late evening is often quite pleasant. And so on. I *allow* the heat, and focus on the elements I can approach from a passionate and loving perspective.

Years ago I had an interaction with the best dentist I have ever encountered. Truthfully, today I have no idea who this man is, and wouldn't know him if he walked through my front door. I was sent to him for an emergency extraction while performing Shakespeare in the Lake Tahoe area. I don't remember if his skill as a dentist was all that great, but here's why I count him as the best ever.

As he prepared to give me the various injections of pain relief medication, he would say to me, "This is going to sting like crazy for about five seconds. Just allow the discomfort, and it will immediately get better." I found myself experiencing the discomfort for a second or two, and then suddenly feeling the relief of the Novocaine, or whatever he was using. Now, previous dentists had always told me, "This won't hurt a bit." And then they stuck a needle in my gums! Of course I would then jerk and spasm in pain, making the injection all the more difficult. Why? Because I had been assured it wouldn't hurt.

When Dr. Tahoe asked me to simply *allow* some discomfort, I found I could easily do it because I was expecting it, and actually found the pain less than anticipated. Brilliant. Allow some discomfort.

On a recent trip to a speaking engagement, I was very much looking forward to my seat in the First Class section of the airplane. It had been a difficult week, and I felt I needed to catch a nap on the lengthy flight so I would be refreshed and ready to go when I arrived at the venue. On a long flight, that little bit of extra legroom and the slightly thicker pillow in First Class makes a huge difference to me; I don't know about you. I politely refused the complimentary champagne that was offered (of which I would normally accept at least one!) because I was ready to settle down for a little shut-eye. In the seat next to me, a well-dressed gentleman took his place. He seemed to be a very nice guy and we exchanged brief hellos and smiles. I buckled up, arranged my pillow and began to drift off. It didn't take long to notice that my seatmate had a very peculiar and disturbing nervous tick. Every 15 seconds he would sniff, sniff, sniff, sniff-sniff, sniiiiiiiifff. Yes, I mean it, every 15 seconds. You could set your watch by it. I tried covering my ears with the pillow. No help. I ordered headphones, plugged them into the airplane's music system. No help.

With each sniff, I found myself becoming more and more agitated, looking around to see if anyone else objected as strongly as I did to this intrusion. No one seemed to notice. I looked imploringly at the flight attendants. They simply shrugged, continuing their duties. What could they do? Soon, I was nearly beside myself and no longer sleepy. All I could concentrate on was my growing annoyance at this uninvited intrusion. Didn't he know he was doing this every 15 seconds? Didn't he realize how annoying it could be to people nearby? Didn't he know I had an important speech to give! It was almost like the famed water torture: drip, drip, drip...

My entire being was consumed with the thought of the outrage of this occurrence. I began plotting solutions, witty comments, a visit to the cockpit to air my grievances (the cockpit!), and all sorts of complex revenge schemes. Of course I did none of them. What good would those things do? And all I had accomplished so far was to work myself into a frenzy that would make me even less effective when I arrived at my destination.

Finally, I recalled my New Rules of Thinking. Yes, sometimes even I forget the power of the New Rules. We think we can change others, or that our outrage will rectify a difficult situation. In that moment, I, like most people, had to take a second to check myself, to get a grip. Initially, I had to return to New Rule of Thinking #4 and find a way to look at this obstacle from a new perspective. Certainly, continuing to become more frustrated, and flashing more looks to the airline staff would not bring a different and satisfactory outcome. So, I began to make the effort to see the situation from a different perspective. How could this interruption be viewed as less of a problem? Could I fix the person next to me? No. Could I allow him his sniffling? Could I release my initial reactions to this annoying habit? Just let it go? Well... perhaps with a new perspective.

I made a personal vow to *allow* the intrusion of my neighbor's sniffing. I began to count sheep using the sound of the sniff as the sound effect of each fluffy sheep barely clearing a wooden fence as I counted them. Sniffff-one; sniffff-two... and so on. Before I even realized it, I drifted off to a very pleasant sleep filled with lovely sheep prancing over an ornate wooden gate. Best nap I've had in some time. All because, instead of objecting to my circumstance, I *allowed* a certain amount of discomfort. Yes, Messrs. Hornsby and Sinatra, sing it again.

There's no need to react violently to every discomfort in life, especially if you know it's coming. In regard to the things which we cannot control, we must allow a small amount of discomfort, and shift our focus to the things that bring us joy and satisfaction. We are obligated to fix what we can; the rest we must allow and release to the universe.

That's just the way it is.

Human beings, by changing the inner attitudes of their minds, can change the outer aspects of their lives.

— William James

NEW RULE OF THINKING #8:
I Will Control The Spiral Staircase

People come to me all the time asking for guidance because they feel their lives are out of control, on a downward spiral. They tell me, "I'm doing the exact same things I've always done, but lately nothing seems to go right. And the more I try to change my results, the worse it seems to get! And don't tell me I'm practicing the insanity of applying the same strategy over and over again! I'M BEING CREATIVE, BUT MY RESULTS DO NOT CHANGE!"

We can all relate to this situation. We see it not only in our own lives, but also in the lives of our favorite celebrities.

Take the example of a Major League baseball player who has been hitting over .300, knocking lots of balls out of the park, and fielding with few or no errors. Then, for no obvious reason, things go south, and just as quickly the player is mired in a slump. The obvious immediate remedy is additional batting/fielding practice. The player dedicates hour after hour to more and more practice balls in a desperate attempt to change the results, and nothing makes a difference.

In another sport, basketball, we see it occur all too often that a star player has every element of his or her game working, but cannot make a free throw to save his or her own life. And, everyone — coaches, teammates, friends, family, fans, taxi drivers, and more — has a suggestion as to how to fix the result: stand farther back, bend your knees more, put more arc on the shot, take less preparation time, and so on. Yet, the results stay the same.

In the business world, it's not uncommon for an executive whose instincts have traditionally been spot on, and whose leadership and courage have led the company to great success, to employ one unfortunate unsuccessful strategy which causes him or her to suddenly come under fire for every ensuing decision. These execs usually make every effort to exact a change: scheduling more meetings, seeking more counsel, exhaustive research, and more. Somehow, none of these tactics gets the "monkey" off the executive's back.

Actors continually report, "Last year was a blockbuster year for me! I worked nonstop, but this year I can't get arrested; and I feel like I'm doing the best work of my career, and giving better auditions than ever."

The point is, obviously, if you have found yourself in this predicament, you are not alone. What is the solution? How can we change our results when everything feels off target? How do we get off this spiral staircase?

It is true, there can be a spiral staircase. One bad action can influence the next, leading to a downward spiral of events that is difficult to stem. But here's the good news:

The spiral staircase goes both ways!

Just as easily as you found yourself spiraling downward, you can turn it around and generate victory after victory, feeling your results and your life going up, up, up.

You can, of course, through inaction, also just stand in the same place. This is what many people do. They have found a "comfort zone" right where they are, in the middle of the staircase, and they are not going to budge. Granted, where they are is not particularly satisfying. It doesn't inspire joy or lead to the fulfillment of their dreams. Instead, it spares that person the discomfort of risk, judgment, and consequence. The view from a static position on the spiral staircase is relatively standard — not exciting, yet not the worst vantage point. And let's be honest, for some people, that's just fine — as long as the staircase isn't headed downward. In truth, though, this kind of settling probably doesn't apply to you because you have proven to be more of a seeker simply by choosing this book.

And from the middle, you get to see a lot of others coming and going, giving you the chance to silently judge those on their way down while you marvel and "ooh and ahh" at the ones on the way up, as you fight off a tiny bit of envy and/or remorse.

How, you ask, do we turn the staircase around? How do we change negative results into positive ones... and begin the ascent?

First we must begin by understanding that *our position on the staircase is not altered by changing our results*. Results are just that: the result of other factors.

In all of the examples above, the individuals who were unable to change their results were highly unsuccessful simply because they were attempting to change the wrong thing. They were working to alter their results rather than addressing the *causes* of those results, very much the way we sometimes medically address *symptoms* of illnesses with pain medications and more rather than seeking to identify the *causes*. Sure, I'd like to cough less, but wouldn't it be smarter to figure out why I'm coughing in the first place instead of simply suppressing the cough? If you've been reading intently, you have learned that it all starts with "I." The downward *or* upward spiral isn't caused by the results. The results are caused by "Me," what is inside your belief system. And, remember, changing that begins with "I."

Let me say that once more. The bad results don't cause the downward spiral. "Me," the part of you that has bought into a faulty belief system, is the cause, and only "I," the very best and wisest part of you, can create the change of direction.

Here's an example:

Suppose you wanted to build a new house. What would be the

first thing you would need? Many people answer this question first saying, "I'd need wood, nails, hammers and saws, and other construction equipment." Then others jump in and shout, "You've missed the *real* first step! You have to draw up a blueprint." That would certainly make sense. You wouldn't right away start sawing and hammering wood without specifications and measurements, guidelines for how to best complete the action of building the house. And it's true, the better that blueprint is prepared, the better your chances of a stunning result. And if you found the action of building the house suddenly on a downward spiral, your first action wouldn't be to change saws or practice hammering repeatedly. You wouldn't attempt to change the action. You would look to the blueprint to see where the problems are occurring. Ahh, but it doesn't begin there.

Because as logical as this seems, there is a very important and often overlooked step *before* the blueprint in building a house. Before you draw up the blueprint, you have to see the house. You have to have a *vision* of just how this structure will look. You have to be able to picture the finished product so clearly that you get a sensation of how you will feel when you see it from a distance; how it will feel to be inside the house. And that mental image must inspire you and excite you to commit the specifications to paper, which will become the blueprint. Without that vision, you find yourself creating an uninspired blueprint that, truthfully, in your heart of hearts, you do not believe can be built or will satisfy the dream that led you to construct the house in the first place. Certainly technical drawings serve a powerful purpose, but if there is no vision behind those blueprints — just imagine a world without visionary architects where every dwelling looks exactly the same—not only will the results be uninspired, but the likelihood of a downward spiral increases. Why?

Well, what is a spiral? A series of causes and effects in which the preceding event has an effect upon the next in a negative or, alternatively, positive manner.

Let's use the house-building example as a metaphor for most everything we do in our lives. If, when you picture the house you want to build, your fears or limited beliefs — thoughts of not being worthy of such a house, or fears of not being able to finish the construction — cause you to doubt you can build the house of your dreams, your vision will be compromised. You will picture it less beautiful, less grand, perhaps even less functional. After all, your "announcer" voice tells you, "You're not a builder. Who are you to think you could possibly construct the perfect home you've always wanted?" In this metaphor, we are assuming you actually have the capability to build things. Just as in your life, there are many things you have begun to doubt you can achieve, when you, in fact, have the necessary skills. Yet, you've compromised all vision. With this compromise, your efforts to draw a blueprint become compromised. The blueprint reflects the doubt and the downscaled expectation of your compromised vision. The blueprint is functional, if not spectacular.

Keep in mind, your vision must be realistic, something within your means, but it cannot be compromised simply because you lack belief in your own abilities, because that, for no good reason, leads to a compromised blueprint. And a compromised blueprint affects your action, doesn't it? I mean, you are working from an uninspired blueprint based upon a compromised vision. Therefore your action is bound to be less than spectacular, isn't it? You'll do the work, however not the way you would if the blueprint was a stunning document based upon a brilliant vision. And, with this adequate yet unspectacular work being done, what can you expect the early results to be? Mediocre at best.

Now, imagine, when you observe these mediocre results, what happens to your vision. Well, certainly your vision has to be diminished even further because all of the doubts and fears you had in the first place have now come home to roost.

They are justified.

In fact, you think, you were foolish to have had even mediocre expectations. Now you have no (subconscious) choice but to lower those expectations still more. After all, the early results have borne out your greatest fears. This lowered expectation necessitates a slight change in the blueprint — a simpler, more basic drawing, so as not to overwhelm the workers. Now the workers are doing the same old basic and standard work, not the stuff of dreams, which then leads to an even less-impressive result. The more you observe these lackluster results, the more you will gradually erode your vision, which was already unspectacular… and the spiral staircase is fully activated: going down!

You can see how an effort to change the result is an ineffective means of halting the spiral — because the result is at the *end* of the chain. Instead, it is absolutely necessary to change not the result, not the action, not the blueprint, but the *vision*.

You have to change your "internal vision," and that starts with "I."

"I" need to change this. And the first step in that change is the adjustment "I" make in what "I" visualize. The blueprint of my success will never turn out the way "I" want without a picture of how the accomplishment will look.

This isn't just a question of wishing and hoping and daydreaming. It's a process of setting your sights on something worthwhile rather than trying to alter your actions and results before the picture is clear. Remarkably, science has demonstrated that your brain cannot tell the difference between a visualized image and reality. A Harvard study taught two groups a simple five-fingered piano melody. One group physically practiced the melody for two hours a day over five days. The other group merely visualized playing the melody. As you can probably guess, the results of the new neurological wiring that took place were almost identical between the two groups.

You see, the baseball player I mentioned earlier hasn't lost the ability to hit the ball, only the ability to see the hit happening, in the same way you cannot build a house you cannot see. There are, of course, factors that cause the deterioration of our skills — age, illness, loss of passion and more — but even in these cases, you will find that a great deal of the problem is the vision.

The actor who enters the audition without the ability to visualize himself or herself inhabiting the role is bound to present a less-inspired version of the character, which leads to a less-than-spectacular reaction from the producers. Now the actor trudges home still unemployed, thinking, "I thought I was a better actor than that!" Now, sadly, the next audition preparation begins with this nagging thought in the artist's mind: "Maybe I'm not as good as the actor who got the job." This changes the blueprint of the prep, which changes what the actor brings to the next audition, bringing about an even less-desirable producer response. Soon the actor is questioning every choice, and in effect his or her very worth.

The chef who enters the kitchen without some mental picture of the delicious dish she or he will create is operating at a severe disadvantage because every step within the creation of the meal will be lessened by the lack of vision, which will diminish the effort and impair the result. Author Alfred Armand Montapert, who wrote the book *The Supreme Philosophy of Man: The Laws of Life*, touted by many as the precursor to the popular book *The Secret*, said it quite well: "To accomplish great things we must first dream, then visualize, then plan... believe... act!"

The fashion designer who sets out to create a new evening gown has to take a moment not only to visualize the finished garment but the way it will move as a beautiful socialite struts through the entrance of a red carpet event. Otherwise, it's just a dress. That deeper vision makes possible the creation of something new and beautiful.

An ancient Chinese proverb says, "The world belongs to those who cross many bridges in their imagination before others see even a single bridge." You have the power to cross those bridges if you will only pause to use your imagination, and dare to embrace what you see.

How would any inventor ever come up with anything new if they just began tinkering at a workstation without any mental snapshot of the device in question as well as the possible positive uses of that device? Author Peter McWilliams said: "To visualize is to see what is not there, what is not real — a dream. To visualize is, in fact, to make visual lies. Visual lies, however, have a way of coming true." Of course he meant "lies" not in the harmful, deceptive manner, but in tricking your mind (which is an immensely powerful tool) into accepting your vision as reality — a *visual* reality, something your brain feels it can actually see — allowing it to begin the almost magical process of manifesting that vision.

All of the people mentioned above share a common process: daring to see the "house" before they begin drawing a blueprint, and daring to visualize it in a more magnificent and unique way than they might have even thought possible a moment before.

And the same is true for you in most everything you attempt! **Because the vision determines the blueprint — the plan of** *action*. And the blueprint largely affects the action, what you physically *do*. Of course, your action determines your early results; and when those initial results are poor, it can't help but impact your ability to clearly visualize a successful result. And, if the vision is faulty, the cycle continues downward, on and on, as you unsuccessfully attempt to alter the results.

It is essential that you see these results are not a true assessment of your capability. They are only an assessment of the actions taken on your *current* vision.

The baseball player's strikeout is not an evaluation of the player's skill as an athlete. It is merely an analysis of this particular at-bat and the events which created it.

The businessman's impaired results do not qualify his or her skill as a company leader, but they do qualify the "headspace" that executive currently occupies.

Psychologists tell us parents are in error when they respond to undesirable behavior in their children by angrily saying, "You're a bad boy!" In truth, the child is not a bad child. The behavior is bad. The child is simply acting out in the way children do, testing the limits of the world. But all of a sudden, the child has feedback from an un-impeachable source, his or her parent, idol, ultimate authority: "I am bad." Now, this isolated incident serves to shape the child's self-image, his personal vision. Once that faulty personal vision is in place, the child creates a blueprint based upon this miscalculation, which shapes actions in step with the faulty blueprint. As expected, these actions yield disappointing results, leading the child to increasingly view *himself* as "bad" rather than the *behavior* as "bad." Before long the blueprint is actually designed to mirror the vision of a bad person.

And you can see that if this spiral isn't aborted, each event in the chain almost guarantees the next event will be even more compro-mised, leading to results of lesser and lesser quality. Unfortunately, while we're in the middle of this thunderstorm, it becomes more and more difficult to see the actual cause and eventually nearly impossible to picture anything but a giant "L" in the middle of our foreheads. Once that scarlet letter becomes the center of our personal vision, it's hard to see anything else.

Soon, it's like a vicious circle; one event decaying the next in an ongoing pattern, which leads us to the feeling that things just can't go right. But things can go right because the moment we recognize the true source of our spiral, *our vision*, we are able not only to halt the erosion, but to create a self-motivating ascension of that same stair-case. Why?

Because it works the same way! An increased, enhanced, clearer vision begets a more inspiring and technically sound blueprint, which inspires a more capable action, which facilitates a more positive early result. One glimpse of those positive early results reinforces and even enhances our vision. "This can really happen!" This increased vision bolsters our blueprint, which brings about a greater, stronger action, which cannot help but lead to a more successful result. And before you know it, you're on a roll, and people around you are marveling at what a phenom you are. And you are! That is, until some event occurs that manages to penetrate your consciousness and alter your vision in a downward direction... if you let it.

How often have you seen a top music recording artist/composer record gold record after gold record and then suddenly produce an absolute turkey, which leads to a series of less-than-spectacular albums, and, sadly, the artist's fall from grace? Has that artist suddenly lost the musical talent that created those previous million sellers? Or has the artist simply descended the spiral staircase because his or her *vision* was poisoned, diluted, or obscured.

In many cases, that vision is affected by people close to us, who mean us no harm whatsoever. Loved ones, business associates, fans, collaborators and others can't resist offering small tidbits of "feedback" that shake our ability to retain the image of the house we wish to build. In fact, most of us would never be thrown by the comments of critics or absolute strangers. What impact could they possibly have upon our vision, blueprint, action and result? But those whose opinions, respect, and admiration mean something to us are able to introduce the tiny seeds of doubt that make us wonder, just for a moment, if our vision is realistic, visionary, or justified. This can happen without our knowing it. We think we are acting upon a powerful vision because we are following the advice of people who care about us. That's why it's important to take a step back and double check our vision, insuring that it is not infested with seeds of doubt.

When we allow those seeds of doubt to lessen our internal vision, the staircase, by law of nature, reverses itself. "Penthouse, going down!"

I suppose if Andy Warhol had asked his friends if a picture of a can of soup would be an iconic piece of art, they would have grabbed a thermometer and sent him to bed with a hot water bottle and a bowl of that very same soup. But Mr. Warhol had a vision that he dared to clarify in his own mind. Then he created a blueprint for its realization and followed that with an appropriate effort. The results... are obvious. Had he listened to his loved ones and pulled the covers up to his chin, the world would have lost a series of very controversial and fascinating works of art.

Now, let's not confuse ourselves by interpreting this to mean we cannot invite or accept the input of others. Obviously there is always room for, and in fact a need for, collaboration, feedback, and evaluation. The key is learning to engage in these processes without a deterioration of our *belief system*... our vision. The greatest athletes in the world have coaches and trainers. Oscar-winning actresses still require directors and coaches. Business executives and political world leaders depend upon the counsel of advisors and staff. It is only when this input brings about a diminished vision of who we are and what we can accomplish that the destructive cycle begins.

Your favorite pro golfer consults with a caddy, prior to attempting the match-winning putt, about angle, speed, external mitigating factors and more. But never in that process is the golf pro revising his or her vision of self, of ability, of worthiness... of putting the ball in the cup.

We have seen it happen, though, many times throughout history. Especially when a phenomenal newcomer finds himself or herself a few strokes ahead in the final stretch, only to discover that a certain Woods, Nicklaus, or Palmer is hot on their heels. You can see the staircase unfolding. The player begins to question, "Am I really capable of competing with this legend?" If the answer comes back anything but a qualified "yes," you'll see the blueprint slightly altered, which changes even the smallest action, and that results in... a missed putt. Of course, one missed putt is not the worst thing in the world, but if that miss magnifies the doubt and alters the vision, you can bet the spiral is about to begin.

Now flash to the pro who is three strokes behind but has been in the winner's circle and the spotlight time after time. The only picture in that golfer's mind is "greatness." A missed putt here or there does nothing to damage the vision of greatness. The less-than-desirable result of hole 12 has no effect upon the upcoming holes. The golfer can literally see the ball rolling and softly falling into the cup. And that's what happens. That powerful vision clears the way for an effective blueprint: perfectly reading the green, the angle, the right club for the shot, the necessary momentum, the steady backswing, the path of the ball... kerplunk! One of golf's greatest stars, Arnold Palmer, said it this way: "Success in this game depends less on the body than strength of mind and character."

Granted, it certainly helps that this pro has experiential evidence of capability. Previous championships. Keep in mind, this moment isn't about championships. This is about sinking a 15-foot putt. Either you have the vision or you don't. In fact, it is not even mandatory that you have evidence of yourself accomplishing the goal. Sometimes merely the fact that it *can* be done is enough to reinforce your internal vision. You can imagine that earning a million dollars before the age of 21 seemed like a pipe dream for most of us until numerous enterprising young internet moguls began doing it on a regular basis. What seemed impossible moments before now has tangible possibility. I can't imagine any of us attempting a triple somersault onto a single high wire if we couldn't first witness artists like the casts of the world famous *Cirque du Soleil* accomplishing it on a nightly basis (twice on Sundays). But once the ceiling of possibility has been shattered, we can harness that possibility to shape our own internal vision.

If you're thinking, "But I could never do that!" then... you can't. If you're thinking, "I'm not athletic enough to pull that off," then... you aren't... because the vision determines the blueprint.

On the other side of the coin, if we allow our thoughts to gravitate to "Well, that's Michael Jordan* who accomplished that feat, and

I would never dare to think I'm Michael Jordan," our internal vision is instantly diminished, limited, and flawed, which will inevitably lead to a lesser course of action, effort, and result. The cycle begins.

You might argue, "I *really am* nothing like Michael Jordan." This is true on many levels, but please remember, I am not asking or expecting you to be like Michael Jordan in any way. Michael Jordan's path, accomplishments, talents, and staircase are his own. This is not about *being* Michael Jordan. This is about making this one 20-foot jump shot— a task many others and perhaps you yourself have done many times (metaphorically).

You, in truth, may never accomplish what Mr. Jordan has on the basketball court, but the fact is, until someone forms a mental picture of equaling and surpassing those achievements, it most *certainly* will never be done. You may not be Michael Jordan on the hardwood, but you have the potential to be your own Michael Jordan in whatever arena your unique gifts beckon you to be. You have to see it, though, in order to design it.

The point here is, you can work on the action all you want, but if you want to change the direction of the staircase, you've got to take control of the image, the internal vision.

Try this simple exercise. Grab a pen and a piece of paper. If you are right-handed, take the pen in your left hand, and vice versa, and quickly attempt to print your name. Do it.

Unless you are ambidextrous, the result is probably not the best-looking writing you've ever seen. Now, you could practice writing your name over and over, and probably improve the result, but it just might take a long, long while to get the results to where you want them.

Now try this:

Repeat the exercise, but first take a moment to visualize your name the way you want it written. Picture each letter, its shape, its angle. See the entire name in its finished form. Now picture your hand

---

* Apologies to any of you who don't know who Michael Jordan is (arguably the greatest professional basketball player of all time).

creating that result. See in your mind how the hand moves to effect the finished product. Visualize yourself effortlessly making it happen. After all, you have a pen, some paper, a hand, and a goal. There is no evidence that this cannot happen. Now, create it.

How does this attempt compare to your first? Is it exactly what you pictured? Possibly not. Our results seldom mirror exactly our preordained pictures. But is it close? Is it a better result than the first? Would this result encourage your future vision of how possible it might be for you to write with your opposite hand? If not, you might need to strengthen your inner vision. On the other hand, if you answered yes, can you see how this result was a product of your enhanced *vision*? Can you see how that vision led to a better game plan, a blueprint of how you might actually accomplish this task? Certainly you see how that blueprint strengthened your action, thus creating a more encouraging result. If this upward "spiral" continued, it wouldn't be long before writing with your opposite hand was a far less daunting task than you might have imagined.

Like most things, it's not magic. You can't wish it, click your heels three times and expect perfect results. There is hard work involved in almost all positive results. But all of the hard work in the world won't alter a downward spiral if your internal vision is impaired. Even if, as you tried this exercise, you found your results weren't what you hoped — perhaps your writing was even worse the second time — you can change that result, not by focusing on the result but by creating a better, clearer beginning vision. You may simply not be in the habit of picturing beautiful results, but you can.

It all starts with "I."

Vision ⟶ Blueprint ⟶ Action ⟶ Result

The important thing is that we must avoid interpreting isolated results in a way that changes (diminishes) our internal vision.

When I first encountered the theory of Creative Visualization, I initially thought all I had to do was picture a Jaguar convertible and one would appear. I kept watching my driveway, waiting for my shiny new vehicle to materialize. After all, I was picturing it with all my might. Where the heck was it?

My underwhelming result changed my vision: "This visualization stuff is for the birds," which changed my blueprint — I set my sights on a nice, used compact, which certainly changed my actions.

The weakness wasn't in the concept. I had left the "I" out of visualization. I had formed an *external* visualization. I hadn't changed anything about how I saw *myself*, only a vision of the result I wanted. My focus on the result made no difference in the events of the staircase, which would have led to an escalating series of compromises, until one day I would have found myself reduced to dreaming of a shiny pair of roller skates.

I needed to visualize myself in that Jag — the steps I would take to make it happen and the actions necessary. Then as positive results came in, I had to strengthen my vision, thus strengthening every event in the chain. That new picture strengthened my resolve because now not only could I see myself in the new car, but I could see the positive returns I'd gain from being in that car: how much better I would feel, how cruising the coast route with the top down would relax me — allowing for more productivity. I also had to address the cost and where the additional funds to finance this car would come from. I began to visualize the new income stream possibilities and what I would do to open these streams. After all, I was willing to make some sacrifices to attain this goal. Suddenly, it all seemed much more possible. Upward staircase.

I love my new Jaguar convertible.

It works that way at the gym. You know how you first think, "I need to get back to the gym and get myself in shape." Then you help yourself to another slice of pizza and think, "Ehhh, what good would it do anyway?" But, if you can just see yourself going to the gym that first time, see yourself doing even the simplest of workouts, and you *actually do it*, take the necessary action for a week or so, sooner than you imagined you'll see or feel the slightest possible result: perhaps a few pounds, a glimmer of a muscle, a slightly trimmer waistline, what previously seemed a distant and unattainable destination seems a bit more realistic. Now you visualize a more aggressive workout, you take that action, and see better results. Soon you find yourself looking forward to your workouts, and before you know it, you've achieved unbelievable results. Before you know it, you're making better nutritional choices, eating healthier foods on a schedule that better suits your metabolism. The staircase continues upward because you feel better, have more energy, think more clearly, and love the attention you're getting now that you look so much better. Going up.

Until... your vision changes... at the holidays, after a minor injury, when your work schedule gets hectic, after an emotional setback, etc.

Obviously, the key is not letting these setbacks alter your internal vision. We can't control the external setbacks. We can work to prevent them, but we can only control ourselves and our own vision. I repeat: the key is not letting these setbacks alter your internal vision.

How do we do that? By seeing that vision repeatedly, more clearly, more splendidly, more confidently, and most of all more realistically each day. Spend the last minutes of each day reviewing these "golden" images of yourself. Picture yourself blueprinting and taking action on the things you would have happen in your life. And, as stated before, keep these pictures realistic. By realistic, I have no desire to limit your visions. Would Mark Zuckerberg have been unrealistic to picture the billions he'd make from Facebook? No, but he had to visualize the blueprint of how he would acquire those billions rather than just picture the bundles of cold cash.

People ask all the time, "Doesn't my vision have to be realistic in order to be possible?" I simply refer them to a quote by author and life coach Chérie Carter-Scott: "Ordinary people believe only in the possible. Extraordinary people visualize not what is possible or probable, but rather what is impossible. And by visualizing the impossible, they begin to see it as possible."

I prefer to believe the best is yet to come from each of us, and that we are capable of accomplishments far beyond our wildest imaginations. The only way we will ever awaken that imagination is to begin the process of dreaming, to rouse ourselves and get to work dreaming, planning, taking action, and garnering results. We control the spiral staircase. We must provide the spark and motivation to move that staircase higher and higher each day, each hour, and every moment.

Is this another way of saying we have to inspire ourselves to achieve our dreams? Perhaps. Because it all begins with "I."

If you want others to be happy, practice compassion. If you want to be happy, practice compassion.

— The 14th Dalai Lama

NEW RULE OF THINKING #9:
I Will Practice Empathy

It's a Tuesday morning, and Karen is late to the office. In Los Angeles most residents have to deal with a common enemy: the 405 freeway, an unpredictable snarl of traffic on which there never seems to be anything but rush hour. Even on a Sunday morning, we fool ourselves into thinking we can cruise from the city to the San Fernando Valley, only to find bumper-to-bumper madness. On a day where you're running late, it's easy for tempers to flare.

Of course, on this particular morning, Karen finds herself behind a vehicle whose driver seems intent upon thwarting her every effort to save time. She is livid and can't wait for that golden opportunity to pull up alongside that driver to give him "the look." You know, the stare that tells him, "You, sir, disgust me. You have no business operating a motor vehicle, obstructing the holy mission upon which I have nobly embarked. I denounce you with my withering gaze and the judgmental shake of my head. Take that!"

Of course, the driver could care less about Karen's "look" and truly has no idea what offense he has committed, and certainly no feeling of responsibility to Karen or her need to make up the minutes she squandered searching for her car keys this morning. Nonetheless, she feels justified and triumphant as she punches the accelerator for two seconds before encountering the next of 40 villains she will vanquish before arriving at her office.

Now fast-forward to a day where maybe things have not gone so well for Karen. Maybe she got news that her daughter is ill, which instantly takes all of the wind out of her sails. Maybe a business meeting didn't go well. If she's a contractor, perhaps she's distraught because her bid wasn't accepted on the job her team worked so hard to earn. Whatever the cause, it's a less-than-happy day, and Karen is feeling vulnerable, sad, and perhaps a bit distracted. That's the exact moment a vehicle pulls up to deliver "the look" to her. It hurts.

She thinks, "What could I have possibly done to deserve this? Can this person not see I am doing the best I can, and that this day of all days is one where I should be given a break?"

And it all comes clear:

We never know what the person who fails to return our smile in line at the ATM is going through. We have no idea what challenges or bad news they have recently encountered. We don't know what circumstances caused the car in front of us to hesitate three seconds before accelerating through the intersection. We cannot read the thoughts of the person who failed to hold the door for us in a busy office building. How could we know that the driver who cut us off is racing to the maternity ward to witness the birth of his child? Or, heaven forbid, answering an urgent call from a local emergency room. We just can't know.

This is why we must practice empathy.

The ancient sage Epictetus once said: "When you are offended at any man's fault, turn to yourself and study your own faults. Then you will forget your anger."

It's important to take a moment and consider the humanity of the people you encounter because our humanity is our greatest gift. Why assume every individual who does not react precisely according to our expectations is an adversary?

Believe me, with the exception of a few sociopaths with serious illnesses, no one sits at home in the morning planning how they will ruin your day by not holding a door or causing you to miss a green light. There's no conspiracy to take you down. Everybody is doing the very best they can. True, everyone is not always keeping your best interest as a primary concern. Nor should it be, especially if they are dealing with a dying relative or serious financial troubles or a nagging toothache. We are each finding our way as valiantly as possible, so a little empathy can be a very valuable tool.

Take a moment to consider the possibility that the people who annoy you most just might have circumstances going on at home or things that occurred in their past which, hidden from view, dictate their behaviors. It's possible their actions are truly the best those individuals can offer under the circumstances. It's called empathy, and a day will come where a little bit of it thrown your way just might help you through a severely challenging day.

For this reason, practice it. Practice empathy the way the greatest basketball players would practice free throws: long and often. The way a magician practices sleight of hand maneuvers, a chef practices knife skills, or an accountant works at the calculator.

Practice until it becomes second nature.

I once heard an old story about a person who was given the opportunity to observe the great artist Pablo Picasso at work in his studio. Hour after hour, Picasso labored away, intently applying brush to canvas, meticulously scrutinizing each stroke. When, at the end of the day, the observer was given the chance to approach the great man, the obvious question was, "What will this painting be?" The response was, "Oh, this is not a painting. I was practicing my circles."

You are never too old or too wise to practice your empathy. Train your mind to reserve judgment until you have considered the empathetic possibilities. Not only will it cause you to treat people better, which will lead to stronger relationships and surprising new opportunities for success, it will enable you to be a happier and more peaceful being. And if someone you treat better passes that empathy forward to two or three others, and those people do the same, perhaps you have become the catalyst of a new culture of kindness and understanding.

Many of you have heard of the famous "Butterfly Effect," a quantum theory that it is possible for the mere flapping of a butterfly's wings in one location to impact the creation of a hurricane thousands of miles away. One action impacts the next and the next and so on. With your New Rule of empathy, you can create a hurricane of *kindness* — not by changing others, but by applying this New Rule of Thinking to your own behavior, your own code of conduct. In the New Rule that states "Always Do The Highest Thing," we discussed resisting firing off a hurtful remark when someone fails to acknowledge us for holding a door for them to pass through. When we employ that New Rule of doing "the highest thing" and we add to it some empathy, a regard for the other person's feelings and best interests, we cannot only avoid sinking to a lower level, but perhaps we might even come up with an action that could inspire that person, change their day for the better, and compel them to show kindness to other people. Before long, the hurricane of kindness will have been created, all because of a simple adjustment in our own reactions and behavior.

Now, by making changes in yourself, you have effected change in your community and perhaps the world. Can you make a difference in this world? A butterfly can.

"I" can.

To become different from what we are,
we must have some awareness of what we are.

— The 14th Dalai Lama

NEW RULE OF THINKING #10:

I Am Who I Think I Am, And I Get What I Expect

We have a tendency to think our vision of who we are is shaped by the feedback of others. But the truth is, our vision of who we are is shaped by "I."

Do you consider yourself intelligent? If you think you're smart, chances are you'll devour new information, books, and articles in a far more passionate way than your neighbor who thinks he's not so smart. Possibly then, you'll participate actively in conversations, and probably eventually learn even more from the discussions you join.

Do you feel like you're attractive? Then you're going to carry yourself in a way that causes others to find you attractive. Do you think you're too tall? You can bet you'll be walking around all day signaling people exactly that message. If you think you're shy, of course you'll hang back at public gatherings and meetings, and on dates and interviews. If you see yourself as a winner, every win you achieve is going to add to that feeling of being a winner, which, of course, is going to impact the kind of effort you make: stronger, faster, smarter. Because you are who you think you are.

I meet so many businesspeople who know in their hearts how extremely capable they are. Yet in the deepest recesses of that same heart, they don't yet believe that they deserve a place at the boardroom table. They become convinced that those perks are for a different breed of people. As a result, they become who they now imagine they are supposed to be: mid-level, unspectacular worker bees. Not because they're not capable, but because they can't help manifesting results based upon who they *think* they are.

Among the most difficult advice I give to people who come to me for coaching is pointing out that they are not suffering from a fear of losing. They are suffering from a fear of success. Fear of winning.

You heard me right — a fear of *winning*.

Why do they fear winning? Because at the end of the day, what they really believe is that they are not star material. They believe they are made from a different raw material than the Warren Buffetts, Brad Pitts, Kobe Bryants and Meryl Streeps of the world. Now please understand, this is not a discussion about talent. There is only one Meryl Streep. And there is only one *you*. You are as unique as a snowflake, a one-of-a-kind miracle of nature. As a result, Meryl Streep's enormous abilities are not a roadblock for yours or mine. There's room in the universe for Meryl's talent plus yours and mine and one billion more. And maybe it's true that the actor I'm coaching is not ready to play the title role in *Sophie's Choice* (as Ms. Streep did so brilliantly). The question is what role is he or she ready to play? Not being ready to embody one of the landmark roles in film history doesn't make my client a loser. It doesn't make him or her less deserving of success. How do we know if Ms. Streep felt she was ready to deliver when she was cast in that role? Thankfully, even if she didn't believe she was ready, she found a way to step up, day to day, and prove to herself that she was capable. Chances are, each new day provided new evidence to her that she was the right woman for the role. The mere fact that she had won the role must have given her a strong starting suggestion that she had the right stuff. But so often we walk around subconsciously hoping we *don't* win because down deep we really don't believe we have the stuff to live up to the responsibility a win would thrust upon us.

We find ourselves secretly hoping to come in second or a respectable third, yet blaming the lack of victory on external factors: our boss, our income, our significant other, our parents.

When all is said and done, we're getting exactly what we expect because we are who we think we are. We *feel* victory will not come because we *see* ourselves as undeserving of victory.

Did you ever notice how the children of successful people or wealthy people or famous people tend to find success, as well? Most of us would assume this happens because daddy or mommy opened doors for that child. But consider this: is it not possible that child was raised in an environment that reinforced the idea of being a winner? It is probable the child grew up with no other philosophy than one that said "I'm a winner." That's all he or she has ever known. Of course, you have to combine that with the issue of access. It's certainly easier to obtain an internship at a prestigious company when dad plays tennis with the CEO every weekend. Let's not kid ourselves into thinking there aren't certain advantages to being born into a successful family. But which comes first, the chicken or the egg? Do the children of less-affluent families have a difficult time gaining success because they have greater challenges? Or does the circumstance of the challenges determine how they see themselves, and therefore impact their beliefs, blueprints, efforts, and results? Please don't let this become a discussion of rich versus poor. That is not the intent at all. And thankfully we can point to countless examples of financially challenged individuals who have achieved great success, and comfortably affluent people who have lived miserable and unrealized lives. I count myself among the former group. My poverty-level-farm-boy upbringing in Pennsylvania showed no promise of success in this world, financial or otherwise. But my parents did a great job of instilling in me the idea that I could be a winner. In fact, they helped me believe there was no challenge I could not overcome. The gift they gave me was the possibility that I could accomplish anything to which I set my mind. Now, for most of my life I took that to an extreme and set out to accomplish everything. Even today, I can't pass by a catalog of college classes without wishing I could enroll and find five or ten new subjects to master. Some of the things I've attempted in my life I truly believe I have mastered. In those areas I have found great success. Why? Because I am who I think I am. In other areas, my inner belief is that I'm pretty good. And the results that I manifest match exactly that belief. Fortunately, there aren't a lot of areas where I think, "I'm terrible at this." But I do have to admit roller skating is one. When you grow up on a farm, there aren't a lot of areas where roller skates are useful. Plus, being from a dirt-poor farm family, there weren't a lot of pairs of skates hanging around waiting to be strapped on. As a result, I simply never learned how. I grew up thinking I just wasn't good at it. It never occurred to me I might have the skills to be a great skater, but never had the opportunity. Whatever the case, that was my core belief. As a result, to this day, roller skates and I do not get along. My body cannot process how to move even one inch on the skates. Which is crazy because in pretty much every other sport known to man, I range from pretty good to excellent.

But roller skating... nothing doing. Is this a measure of my ability or my belief?

By now the answer should be clear. Take a moment and think what the answer must be. Also try to anticipate what you think became my story with ice skating, surfing, skateboarding, and other "balance sports."

You probably hit it right on the head. Even now, I can't stay on a boogie board in the ocean to save my life. Why? Because I told myself the lie early on that I didn't have those balance skills... and I became who I thought I was. And I will stay that way until I tell myself a different truth (and take the time to master the necessary skills). But it all begins with "I."

In fact, I can tell you, by the time you finish this book, I will have laced up a pair of roller skates, visualized myself cruising down the Venice Beach boardwalk, made the decision that my athletic abilities enable me to conquer any sporting activity, done the research on the how and the why, and proved to myself who I really am: a human being as capable as any other of enjoying the sensation of traveling by roller skates. (See you at the beach! Or on YouTube!)

Whoever we tell ourselves we are, whatever we tell ourselves we can or cannot do, that is what we will manifest. I'm not asking you to tell yourself you're something you're not. Quite the contrary. I'm only asking you to evaluate who you are in a rational and authentic manner. If you're telling yourself you *can't* roller skate — you don't have the skills or the smarts — simply because you've never tried, you're feeding yourself erroneous information and doing yourself a huge disservice. There's no need for "can't" in that assessment. Maybe you even go the next step and label yourself as unathletic. But is that really the case? Or have you just not had the opportunity, the training, the practice, the desire, the time to pursue the skills required to master that particular endeavor? This would apply whether it's math, or cooking, or auto mechanics, building romantic relationships, public speaking and so on. In any of these cases, why label yourself as "unable" or "not a winner"? That's not your authentic truth. And if, after trying, you find you're really not gifted in this area, that's okay. You tried, and now you know. It doesn't make you a loser.

Let's take the bumblebee for example. Fire up your computer and search "bumblebee." Click "images" and take a good look at the construction of this creature: big stocky body, tiny little paper-thin wings. If it were an airplane, you'd be thinking, "There's no way this thing will ever get off the ground." If you click back on your online "bumblebee" page, you'll see essays, arguments, blogs, theories, and more going back and forth on whether the bumblebee is a miracle, a freak of nature, a mistake, or a triumph of will. But whether it can be explained or not, whatever those experts and geniuses say, Mr. Bumblebee will fly. Why? Because he believes he can. He bee-lieves. Because he doesn't read blogs and magazines that would have him think his body is too heavy to take flight. He has wings. He thinks he is meant to take flight... and he does. Think about it. If the bumblebee allowed himself to consider the probability of his body actually taking flight, if he allowed himself to entertain the idea of doubt, he would never get off the ground. Isn't that what we sometimes do to ourselves? We make the decision about what is not possible long before we attempt to make something happen. Fortunately, the bumblebee is a part of nature. He doesn't question whether he should be able to or whether he can take flight. He simply trusts the natural order of things. And instinct tells that bumblebee it's his duty to move from flower to flower, making a crucial difference in the way our world unfolds. He is who he thinks he is. And fly he does, making it possible for almost every other living being to continue the cycle of life.

By the way, if you have a few extra minutes, take a look at some of the articles discussing how the near extinction of bees may lead to a global food shortage of huge proportions. But, that issue is not a crisis of bumblebee faith. Nor can the stumbling blocks in your life afford to be caused by a false view of who you really are and what you truly are capable of accomplishing.

The truth is: you get what you expect.

I know it sounds silly but it really is true. You get what you expect. Sometimes in life we find ourselves actually *expecting* not to win. Maybe it's because we are preparing ourselves for the worst-case scenario. Maybe it's because we get to a point where we find it difficult to truly believe we can win. But in any event, before we know it we are expecting mediocre results. And once we begin expecting them, that's exactly what we get. This has nothing to do with the choice of fear we mentioned earlier. Neither is it the product of focusing on "don't." This is simply what we have come to anticipate our results will be — regardless of our preparation and skill. Deep down we just don't expect to win.

Surely you've had this happen to you: you're buttering a slice of bread or stacking items on the kitchen counter and you say to yourself, "I know I'm going to drop this facedown" or "That's going to fall." Then it happens just the way you predicted. Are you psychic? Did you see the future? Or more likely, did you create that very eventuality?

It's not magic. Every thought that is in your mind has an impact on the behavior you create, which then has a direct impact on the results you achieve. You didn't magically forecast that ruined snack or that kitchen spill. You simply created a circumstance in which they were very likely to happen. You programmed your own behavior to make that result a likelihood. It's not conscious, it's subconscious. And I'm not claiming to be qualified to understand the nuances of the subconscious. In truth, I'm not sure anyone is qualified to do that. That's how complex and mysterious the subconscious mind is. But I do think I'm smart enough, and you're smart enough, to figure out that the things we program in our subconscious tend to lead to the results we create. You get what you expect.

Hopefully you see the subtle difference between "You are who you think you are" and "You get what you expect." While they definitely go hand in hand, they differ in that the former is a question of what you think about *yourself* — who and what you are — while the latter concerns the *results* you have come to anticipate.

Some days you wake up with dread thinking, "This is not going to be a good day." And sure enough, things start to go wrong. Have you ever noticed that when something technical goes wrong, let's say your computer or something with your car or another piece of equipment you own, other things start to go wrong, as well. Your friends who are astrology buffs will tell you Mercury is in retrograde, or the moon is full and the tides are shifting. Okay. I'm sure that's very possible. But isn't it also possible that your expectations set the table for behaviors on your part that led to the day not going as well as it could have?

Don't we usually find that the problem with the computer is something we did or failed to do — the file we didn't back up or memory limit we exceeded? The problem with the car could have been avoided had we not missed our two-year checkup. These are not mystical occurrences. This is cause-and-effect, and in truth, we're getting exactly what we expected, even unknowingly. Why unknowingly? Because the subconscious impacts the conscious thought. This is why it is crucial that we make a definite and specific conscious choice to expect victory. Otherwise, those subconscious seeds of doubt get the opportunity to grow. If you don't make a purposeful decision about what you *want* to grow in your garden, cultivating and nurturing that choice while weeding out the rest, you make room for any and every weed blowing in the wind to take root.

The single greatest development in my personal life came as a result of the first time I realized that I was expecting to win. Since that day, my life has become one incredible victory after another. I don't attribute that to the fact that I'm so great or so smart or so talented because I think these victories are available to everyone. The difference is I wake up each day honestly expecting to win. In fact, it's shocking to me when I don't win. It really puzzles me.

I exclaim, "How is this possible? Something must be wrong here because I am supposed to win!" The more I expect victory, amazingly, the more victory I receive. Is it magic? Well, I have to admit it feels like magic, but the New Rules tell me it's simply a result of getting what I expect and deserve.

What if you were able to take control of your expectations? What if you really could interpret your previous results and other data in a way that caused you to expect to win, to expect success? I suppose a lot of people would just call that "positive thinking." But what I'm talking about is more than positive thinking. I'm talking about the *expectation* of a positive result, a new feeling about what will come and therefore a new attitude, energy, and course of action.

Imagine you're in the locker room of a professional sports team at halftime and the coach steps up to the blackboard and says, "Well, boys, we know we're not going to win this, so here's how we're going to make that happen." Then he proceeds to diagram a set of plays that will ensure the loss he predicted. What do you think the result is going to be?

We run the plays that are diagrammed. And who is in charge of drawing up those game plans? We are. "I" am.

If that coach had employed the "different perspective" New Rule of Thinking to see the dilemma in a different way, perhaps he or she might have seen a possibility that would tighten up the defense and limit the number of points the opposing players would score in the second half. Now with that possibility in mind, the coach might have seen that if these new measures were carried out, he or she could confidently expect a victory. And in expecting a victory, that coach's feeling might have inspired a behavior in his players that would reinforce the winning game plan, leading to the realization of that winning expectation. For those who would ask if a positive expectation *always* leads to victory, I would refer you to the earlier chapters: there is no always. Furthermore, in truth, a coach's true objective cannot be focused solely on victories and defeats, but rather on the quality of the effort, the teamwork, the learning, and the experience. While the scoreboard may not always reflect a "win," these other factors can certainly provide the kind of victories that will accomplish the actual life objectives, and therefore eventually, the win.

Sometimes it's as simple as a situation in which you have decided to approach your supervisor with a new idea you really believe will help the company by improving productivity. But you know this person to be a tough cookie. Without realizing it, you go into the meeting with the feeling, the expectation of being shut down… and sure enough, that's what happens. It's not mystical. Your expectation has a direct impact on the spirit in which you present your new idea. If that spirit causes your body language or your tone of voice to say, "You're probably going to hate this, but here goes," the less-than-stellar result is almost inevitable. Did you purposely bring that attitude to the room? Of course not. You probably didn't even know you did it. But your expectation determined your vision and blueprint, which determined your effort, and the result was almost inevitable.

I repeat, I get that we've all heard about and possibly misunderstood creative visualization many times. Picture that shiny new bicycle and it will appear. That's not what I'm talking about. I'm talking about your expectation, your feeling. What you expect and how you feel influences what you plan. And what you plan influences what you do, and the way in which you do it. On any given day, I know I'm capable of various levels of effort. Some days I bring my "A" game, and other days, sadly (because my "A" game is so much more effective, fun, and in line with who I really am), I bring my "B" game. Why a different quality of game on different days? Different game plan. Why a different game plan? Different expectation. Why a different expectation? Violation of the New Rules.

If you want to win, expect to win.

If you walk around saying, "With my luck, this will never happen," then nothing is ever going to happen. If you walk around predicting negative results, without you knowing it, your subconscious is quickly getting to work bringing about those very results. As the author Dorothea Brande wrote: "Envisioning the end is enough to put the means in motion."

I'm not asking you to walk around wearing rose-colored glasses and blurting out positive greeting card quotes all day long. I'm asking you to utilize the New Rules to see your day in a different way, and process that information in a manner that allows you to expect a positive result.

You may ask, "What do I do when I don't win? What happens when I keep coming up short? I start out expecting to win, and still I lose. What now?"

This is simple. Go back to New Rule of Thinking #4. Chances are, if you're expecting to win but you're applying the same strategies, you're practicing insanity. Try looking at the task at hand from a new perspective, allowing you to see a new strategy, a new game plan, and an even stronger expectation.

Before you know it, you'll be winning because, if you are steadfast in using the New Rules to your best advantage, you get what you expect.

You must remember there's that voice in your head reinforcing every negative idea you grasp, feeding it to your subconscious, whether or not that idea is valid or true.

Some of you would ask if this New Rule can lead to a lack of humility, encouraging arrogance. Let's be clear: your humility is found in how you treat other people. In knowing how great you are, you will find no need to inform or convince others of that greatness. You will avoid any actions that might make the person next to you feel smaller in comparison to your own excellence. In fact, you will use that excellence to uplift and encourage the people in your circle: the ultimate humility. But how will you be able to provide encouragement to anyone if you have convinced yourself that you are not capable, not powerful, not heroic or worthy? You must, as the airline crews tell us in the event of a sudden depressurization, "Put your own mask on first;" then you will be strengthened to help others who may be in distress. Save your humility for the moments you interact with others, but get to work understanding and embracing who you really are.

You have to be careful what you think about yourself, what you say about yourself, what you feel and believe about yourself. Because we truly are who we think we are.

Who do you think you are?

Well... what did you expect?

*There's only one corner of the universe
you can be certain of improving,
and that's your own self.*

— Aldous Huxley

NEW RULE OF THINKING #11:

I Will Believe In Myself, And Convince Others To Do So As Well

Often I ask my clients, potential employees, and students what their knockout punch is. They look at me like I've asked them to provide the cure for the common cold. Remember our boxer? Why on earth would he ever enter the ring without an absolute knowledge of his ultimate strength, the move that is going to assure his victory? If you're running around the ring trying to avoid your opponent's haymaker, what, beyond extreme good fortune, is going to bring you victory? You *have* to know where your power lies! Imagine how much easier it would be to fully believe in yourself if you clearly understood and appreciated the source of your strengths. Conversely, think how counterproductive it is to charge into battle with no clear sense of those advantages. If you have millions of dollars tied up in real estate (or hundreds of dollars in a neighborhood fundraiser), you can't be making decisions designed to avoid losing any money. You have to have a vision of the proactive championship techniques that will make your investment a success. And you have to put those actions into effect. You have to believe in your strengths and throw the knockout punch!

Is your knockout punch your intelligence? Then you must get in position to end the match by applying those smarts in a decisive fashion. Is it your charm? Same approach. Your exhaustive preparation, sincerity, your disarming humor, cool under pressure, your revolutionary idea, your ability to assemble the right team, your devastating beauty? Whatever is your ultimate equalizer, you must have a knowledge of it and be ever vigilant, searching for the chance to win with it.

So many of the dreamers I meet are reluctant to talk about their strengths because they have been taught that this will be perceived as arrogance. Certainly if you strut around announcing unsolicited how wonderful you are, that will smack of arrogance. But what we're talking about here is a salesperson's knowledge of the product. Suppose you go to a car dealership to purchase a new car and you ask the salesperson, "Is this a great car?" Now suppose the salesperson shrugs his or her shoulders, shuffles their feet, and says, "Aw shucks." Would you want to buy that car? Heck no. You'd want to hear the amazing strengths this vehicle has to offer, the extras, the luxuries. And it's the salesperson's duty to know what those strengths are and to point them out to you.

The same is true for us.

Because whether we like it or not, the pursuit of success is largely sales. We always have to convince someone else to buy into our idea, our strategy, our dream, our product — even if that product is ourselves. It begins with belief... in "I."

What good would the personal computer be if the pioneers had not been able to sell others on the idea that its technology could change their lives? We both know that's a pretty easy sell... today. Was it so easy years back when the functions were more primitive, the size enormous, and the costs far higher? Truth is, *your* sales pitch needs to be an easy sell as well. Not arrogance. Not cockiness. Just an unabashed *knowing* of what the strengths of your product, your position, or your approach really are.

And it goes beyond simply knowing. In most situations, it includes needing to be able to *articulate* those strengths in a concise manner that clarifies your necessary actions, and, in turn, silences would-be critics.

Many people call it "The Elevator Speech."

The idea here is, suppose you stepped into an elevator on the first floor of a high-rise and punched floor 15, only to discover that you were alone in the elevator with the one person in the world who could assure your ascension to the "next level" of success. Now imagine that person turns to you and says, "I like to give opportunities. Why should I give you one?"

DO YOU HAVE AN ANSWER?

Well, you now have 15 floors to come up with one and deliver it.

Perhaps you are an up-and-coming salesperson hoping for an opportunity to get the ear of any substantial buyer, but those opportunities have not yet appeared. The passenger with you is the chief buyer from the largest merchant of the product you represent. You have 15 floors to make an impression.

Or you are a young screenwriter and the passenger is Steven Spielberg. Will you spend the first five floors telling him what he already knows? "Hey, you're Steven Spielberg." It gets worse: "I love your movies!" Seventh floor; eighth floor... remember, he has told you "I LIKE TO GIVE OPPORTUNITIES." This is no time for platitudes. This is time for action. Are you prepared?

Are you a university campus parking lot attendant who is capable of much more than your current position affords? Your passenger is the head of HR at the university. What will you say?

Or, the person of your romantic dreams steps into the elevator and punches the "15" button when you notice the conspicuous absence of a wedding ring on the left hand, and a match.com printout tucked beneath the right arm. "Going up." The clock is ticking, and your house with a picket fence and 2.5 children is about to step off at floor 15. Is there something you should say?

If you're walking around your city without a well-prepared paragraph that can be articulated before you reach the 15th floor, you are not prepared for an opportunity to change your life.

Your elevator speech is not easy to craft. It's very difficult. It has to be succinct. It cannot be common; claims that have been uttered many times before will not do the trick. It wants to be confident without being cocky. It has to be something that will instantly and ultimately appeal to the target, and it must be something upon which you can genuinely deliver. If you spend the rest of your career shaping this message, it will be well worth your time. A great elevator speech will take you a lot higher than the 15th floor.

Keep in mind, it doesn't have to include super-human powers, although that would be fantastic if you could deliver on such a claim. As stated before, it can be as simple as absolute sincerity, if that is a strength you can convert to actual value. Humor, for example, in and of itself may not be a unique or viable strength, but coupled with the ability to diffuse pressurized situations, it becomes an invaluable asset.

In my career as a director of live and filmed events, I found time and time again that my employers wanted me on the job because I could remain calm in "crunch time." When all others on the set or in the venue were losing their heads and the screaming and shouting began, I had the ability to remain calm, find solutions, and restore order, resulting in a successful production. I learned that this is a skill that fits well in an elevator speech because nothing derails a production faster than panic and mutiny. Of course, I had to back that up with some creativity and leadership skills, but the point is lots of my competitors could claim creative skills with many more credits than mine to back it up. I had to be armed with something greater to distinguish why my employers needed me.

What is your elevator speech? Do you have it down? If you do, does it work? Have you tested it on friends and associates, or better yet, on potential benefactors?

If not... time to get to work. Don't be modest while you shape it. Find the essential strength, and then build humility into your speech.

And remember, if it takes longer than the 1st floor to the 15th, it's too long. Obviously, many people will need more than one elevator speech, depending upon who gets in the elevator, but let's start with the one that speaks to your greatest and deepest desire. Let's make sure *that one* is covered.

Going up!

Men's natures are alike;
it is their habits that separate them.

— Confucius

NEW RULE OF THINKING #12:
I Will Determine My Habits

Here's an important question: what is your best habit? You know what I mean, your best habit — the thing you do pretty much every day almost as a reflex. It's something you do that you hardly have to think about. It's just something you always do.

Some people, when I ask them, say exercise — "I exercise every day." Others mention prayer — not a day goes by that they don't engage in some kind of prayer. One important executive I know says he spends a few minutes reviewing the previous day, finding the moments that were important and ones he would like to improve. Other people say they take a moment of gratitude at the start of the day. For some people it's making their bed; it's just an automatic thing they do every day.

You may wonder why I ask. Well, it should be obvious to all of us that your habits help determine who you become. The things you do on a daily basis lead you to where you are and what you accomplish. A great pianist doesn't simply become a great pianist through osmosis. It's practice. It becomes a habit. Usually not a day goes by that a great musician doesn't spend some time playing his or her instrument of choice.

A Las Vegas blackjack dealer learns to manage the game, dealing cards, paying off bets, scooping up chips all through the repetition of habit. I'm sometimes asked why I scream at the television set when I see a professional basketball player miss a free throw. The reason is that I believe a pro player should not miss a free throw. Why? Because by the time you become a professional in that game, you have to have shot so many free throws in your lifetime that making the shot should be a habit. For the average person, this shot is a question of chance, odds, and even luck. For a professional for whom this motion has become a habit, those factors are far less impactful.

We all have certain habits. We all have things that we do almost by reflex. The question I would ask is what habits do you have that are leading you to the success you want in your life? What do you do on a daily basis that you know is moving you closer to your dreams? That habit doesn't always have to be a big thing. Sometimes it's something very small that becomes part of your daily routine, yet it slowly inches you closer to the place you hope to arrive. If my dream was to achieve a level of good health and muscularity, even 10 to 15 push-ups a day, every day, out of habit would eventually get me to a physical state that I would find rewarding. If I were a novelist, even writing three pages a day, no matter what the content, would probably put me in the right frame of mind to create my Great American Novel. But it would have to become a habit.

What we do out of habit shapes who we become and what we accomplish. The good news is you're in charge of your habits. You have the ability to choose what your daily repetitive activities will be. What could you choose right now that would effectively bring your dreams a little closer to fruition?

Choose your habits.

By the same token, we probably need to take a look at what habits we have that get in the way of our success. For most of us, there are things we do that we know are not conducive to our prosperity. But they are habits. We do them almost without thinking. And they become a part of who we are.

It's a good time to ask what habits we could eliminate from our daily routine that, by getting rid of them, we just might make building a successful and rewarding life a little easier. Because, once again, we are in charge of our habits. We have the power to shape our own lives.

Would cutting out cigarettes make your journey a little easier? Is it one less drink? Perhaps we could cut out the tendency to judge others. Or the instinct to blame ourselves, to put ourselves down, to choose fear instead of love. Many times these harmful behaviors are just habits — things we do simply because we've done them repetitively for so long, we do them without thinking.

Today would be a great day to take control of your habits. To choose new habits that you know will bring you success and fulfillment. To identify the habits that are not helping you move forward, and cut them out of your daily routine, and out of your life.

Someone very wise once said, "Old habits die hard." And that may be true, but even more true is the idea that we build habits one day at a time. Why not start today?

Remember the gym example? I know it's true for me when I make the decision that I want to get myself back in top physical shape, I have to drag myself to the gym. Those first three weeks are very difficult and often very painful. Many times along the way I find myself wanting to come up with excuses why I can't go. But if I can regularly make myself get to the gym and begin my workout, after approximately three weeks it simply becomes habit. In fact, I find I get to the point where it feels strange not to go to the gym. And before I know it, my physical condition has improved dramatically. And the improvement in that condition encourages me to get to the gym more often and have a better workout each time. I admit it's difficult to find the time, the energy, the motivation to get myself to work out on a daily basis. But once I decide it's going to become a habit, after a few weeks of regular commitment, it really does become a habit. And my habits shape who I've become, what I accomplish, and what success I've achieved.

What habit will you choose? Is it physical? Is it behavioral? Is it emotional? Is it simply making sure your shoes are shined on a daily basis? And will that lead you to success? Well, it just might allow people to see you in a more professional and self-loving light. But you don't have to choose shining your shoes.

It's your life. It's your dream. It's your habit.

Choose wisely.

We must have strong minds,
ready to accept the facts as they are.

— Harry S. Truman

NEW RULE OF THINKING #13:

I Will Stop Asking A Question Once It Is Answered

Have you ever spent the day with a three year old — answering the same questions over and over and over? It doesn't matter how many times you answer, three year olds will keep asking until they get the answer they want — or, as most parents know, until they are distracted by something more interesting, which leads to a whole *new* set of questions. But whether or not the child gets the answer he or she wanted, the toughest questions of all follow: "Why?" "But why?" "But why not?" "But I want it!" "Can I have it?" "Why?"

We're not three year olds. (Unless you are the first 36 month-old I've ever met who can process philosophical literature. If so, I bow down to you.)

As a result we should be able to process a reasonable answer and hold on to it as useful data. But how many times do you find people around you constantly seeking reassurance about questions that have long since been answered?

Every other year, I'm called in to coach a corporate CEO in preparation for the opening address of his company's worldwide seminar. When I first arrive, I find the executive's anxiety level at maximum. "I'm not a public speaker," he says. "Maybe I should just cancel the speech or have someone else do it." And every year the same thing happens: we get to work finding the most powerful points within his speech. We discuss his goals, and why he wants to communicate those important points. Once he has focused on his true intent, it becomes apparent that he really is passionate about the information he wants to convey. Once we tap into that passion and give him a clear image of who it is he wants to inspire and why, he finds himself less and less in need of the printed page and more and more confident about the message he has to share. Before long, he's adding inspired thoughts that have occurred to him during our practice sessions, and improving the message and content of the speech dramatically. Truthfully, in our sessions I find myself extremely inspired by his message, his passion, and his leadership.

Now, I'd love to tell you he charges into the seminar and blows the audience away with those attributes. But the truth is, his seminar speech, while great and inspirational, is never as powerful as it was in the practice room with me. Why? Because the questions are still in his head: "Can I pull off this speech? Am I a public speaker? Will anyone be inspired by me?" And as long as those questions are in his head, his vision and his blueprint will undermine his action in the most subtle or perhaps extremely profound ways.

The question has already been answered. It was answered in that practice room. As a result, it doesn't need to be asked again.

"Can I pull off this speech?"

Well, if he could put a lump in the throat of a tough critic, public-speaking coach like me, he absolutely has the power to inspire his team members. The question has been answered.

There is no value in continuing to re-ask questions to which you already have the answer. If a courtroom judge questions his or her *ability* to fairly preside over the proceedings in that room every time a new case is presented, the judge is reinventing a wheel that has already long since been invented. The question of whether he or she can perform these duties is not a valid question. It's been answered. Certainly, it's reasonable to ask, "Can I be consistent?" "Will I be at my best today?" Reasonable and important questions. But it's equally important that the answers to those questions are based upon authentic data because my fellow CEO friend isn't basing his insecurities upon past results. He is simply repeating and reinforcing his *fears* from the past. And his past results have been successful! So he is revisiting issues that have already been addressed, confronted, and conquered. To ask those questions again is counterproductive and damaging.

I want to make it clear that I'm not suggesting throwing caution to the wind. We must always be conscious and cognizant of our circumstances and the challenges before us. These are reasonable considerations. But when we question our ability, our value, our chances of success, it's essential we take a moment to determine whether these questions have already been answered. Because to waste time wrestling with those questions distracts us from the real question which is, "What must I do to achieve success in this moment… now?"

When the family gathers around the birthday girl watching her open gifts, and she opens the box containing the bracelet she's had her heart set on, and she jumps from her seat screaming and running in place, "Do you like it?" is a question that doesn't need to be asked. It's rhetorical. It's merely a device we use to direct more gratitude and good feeling to ourselves as the giver of the gift. Isn't this a moment where the good feeling should be directed toward the recipient? It's a question that has already been answered. I'm not trying to tell you what to do at birthday parties, only to remind you, as our judge friend hears every day, "Asked and answered, Your Honor."

So, please understand, this is one example of the thousand questions we ask that have very little useful purpose. This one birthday example may not cause a great deal of harm, but there are other questions you may be asking yourself that negatively impact the important life decisions you make, the efforts you contribute, and the results you achieve. In these circumstances, it's important to make sure those questions are productive and fresh because the old questions are simply a retread of past fears, insecurities, and results that have since been improved. Questions such as, "Can I give a speech in front of 100 people?" "Can I propose a touching toast at a dinner party?" "Am I smart enough to join in the cocktail-hour conversation?" and others of this ilk are a waste of time and energy once you've previously accomplished the tasks in question. What's the point fretting and suffering over the next toast once you've proven it can be done? Certainly you want the next toast/speech/conversation to be better each time, but the fundamental question has been answered and need not be raised another time.

Let's go a step further while we're talking about retreading past questions and experiences. There is an important theory that states that universal justice demands we acknowledge our mistakes and atone for them only once. It is cosmically unfair to continue being punished repeatedly for transgressions we have acknowledged and attempted to rectify. (Yes, even the darkest deeds, if the punishment fits the crime, should be atoned for only once, though that punishment may last years or lifetimes.)

Yet, I personally, continually, find myself flinching as I review something that happened way back in the fifth grade; an embarrassing moment, an act that was committed of which I'm ashamed, a foolish or hurtful statement I made. I have an actual physical reaction as if the event had just occurred, even though it happened decades ago. What I'm really doing is punishing myself numerous times for being wrong, for not being good enough, for doing a bad thing. But how does that serve me?

The New Rules of Thinking have taught me there is no value in this. What I really need to do is take a moment and see if I have honestly made a genuine effort to undo the wrong that was done. Now, that can be pretty difficult when it's something that happened in fifth grade. But did I do the best that I could do, and make every effort to undo any harm that may have been inflicted? Have I learned from the mistake that was made? If so, universal justice says the punishment should stop. You may ask, "What if the transgression was something very serious which caused a great deal of harm to myself or others? What if my behavior was despicable?" The key here is making sure you have done everything you can to own up to and apologize for the wrong you did. Is there some reparation you can make, in some way, to right the wrong? If so, do it, and the rule remains: one mistake, one acknowledgement, one punishment. Done.

You can stop beating yourself up.

Shift your focus to creating more good and a more enlightened "I."

Regardless of how you feel inside, always try to look like a winner. Even if you're behind, a sustained look of control and confidence can give you a mental edge that results in victory.

— Arthur Ashe

NEW RULE OF THINKING #14:
I Will Become A "Success Magician"

Here's where you're probably scratching your head. You're thinking, "Hasn't he been telling me throughout this entire book that it's not magic? And now suddenly he's asking me to become a magician? And what the heck is a *Success Magician?*" Well, as any good magician will tell you, pulling a rabbit out of a hat is not magic. It involves a lot of preparation, misdirection, and showmanship. Not to mention raising a bunny.

You see, what a magician does is give you exactly what you want. You want to be astonished. You want to believe something magical has taken place. Through a process of misdirection — shifting your attention to exactly the place he or she wants you to focus, allowing him or her then to make changes in the areas where you are not focused — the magician is able to seemingly make things appear and disappear, read your thoughts, and even predict future events. But as you may have guessed, what is really happening is the playing out of events that have already been predetermined. A lot of the *success* you hope to achieve in your life, your career, and your relationships involves exactly the same process. Thus the new term "Success Magician." A person who makes the things people are hoping to see, the elements that lead to success, appear— as if by magic.

Think about it. When you go on a job interview, you're meeting with a person who wants nothing more than to find the perfect candidate. After all, the sooner he or she finds a qualified person to fill the position, the sooner he or she can get back to the hundred other tasks stacked up on the desk. We genuinely hope and pray that the person who answers our needs will be the next one who walks through the door. That person can be you, but it requires a few magician techniques.

Like a capable magician, you need to ask yourself what does my audience want to see; what do they want to experience? Well, on a job interview, obviously they want someone capable, trustworthy, dynamic, and team-oriented, for starters. Plus, depending upon the job, probably a handful of other outstanding attributes. The truth is, they hope to notice these things within the first minute of the interview. It's in that crucial first minute where decisions are made. First impressions, the scholars and poets tell us, are the most lasting. In other parts of your life, it might be true that those decisions are made over time. You have friendships and relationships that have taken years to develop. But in the job market, we do not enjoy the luxury of time to build relationships. We want what we want, and we want it now. And your job is to deliver. But there is a bit of prestidigitation involved here. Let me give you an example:

Not too long ago, I was invited to a dinner party at the home of some dear friends. For entertainment, these friends had engaged a magician who roamed the party performing really impressive and entertaining tricks for small groups during the cocktail hour. One trick in particular was a crowd favorite. The magician would take a deck of playing cards and hold it at eye level in front of a guest. He would then riffle the deck quickly, asking the subject to watch the cards and choose one card during the three seconds that the 52 cards appeared. Each participant would choose one card he or she had seen and keep it in mind. Miraculously, the magician would, without hesitation, verbalize the card that had been chosen. For example, the three of diamonds. Magic?

I think you and I can safely agree there's an explanation to how the illusion was executed. Obviously, our first guess would be that there was more than one three of diamonds in the deck. It only *appears* we were choosing the three of diamonds randomly, when in fact through subliminal persuasion, the magician was convincing us to select that card. Once we choose the three of diamonds, we are amazed at his ability to give us exactly the answer we were hoping for.

But that's not magic.

And a job interview, for example, is not magic either. We've already identified the qualities an interviewer is seeking. Now all we have to do is "stack the deck" with glimpses of those qualities, flashing them casually so that our interviewer will think he or she alone has identified those qualities. As the interview continues, they become more and more impressed and astonished at how all of the qualities they hope to find are appearing before their very eyes.

What are we talking about here? We're talking about the things you do that subconsciously say, "I am trustworthy," "I am organized," and so on. In the same way the magician flashes the three of diamonds to his subject, our responsibility is to flash the things our audience needs, subtly so as not to be caught doing it. Certainly, the audience wouldn't go wild if the magician shouted, "Choose the three of diamonds," and then guessed, "Is your card the three of diamonds?" It must be subtle, occurring almost undetected, and yet it must be clear and powerful enough to penetrate the consciousness of your subject. Well, how hard is that to do on a job interview?

What are the subtle behaviors a potential employer needs to see in order to be convinced a candidate has the qualities we mentioned earlier? It's not rocket science. And yet, so many job applicants are focused primarily upon their *own* comfort, their *own* needs, and their *own* accomplishments. That would be like the magician guessing the card he himself wants to see, which certainly wouldn't excite audiences, and it wouldn't look like magic. Certainly, it's important for the applicant to be comfortable — but it must not be the first priority.

Let's be clear, there's no trickery here. This is not deception. This is giving the people in front of you exactly what they want and what they need. There's no guesswork involved.

When I speak about the magic of success, I'm always reminded of a reality television show that was on the air some years back called *Blind Date*. The premise was that a contestant would agree to go on three dates, each with a different person, and by the end of the show that contestant would choose which person with whom he or she would like to have a second date. It never ceased to amaze me, the different dates these couples would go on. I mean, almost 80 percent of the time, the guys competing to win chose an activity that they wanted to do. For example the, pro golfer would take his date golfing. Now, we can see he loves golf, but his date doesn't. So what does the evening become but a chance for him to show off his skills, his passion for the game, while placing himself in his own comfort zone? If this contestant had only taken a moment to consider her comfort level, choosing an activity she would enjoy, he might've had a chance to speak to her heart, to make the evening a memorable one that might not only lead to the prizes offered by the reality show, but perhaps a relationship he would value for a lifetime. Very often, going into these important interactions, we shift our focus to ourselves, to "Me." We worry about how we are doing, and how we are feeling, and what the other person is thinking of *us*, when we should be simply flashing the three of diamonds as quickly, subtly, yet pervasively as possible.

When, on your blind date, you hear your partner mention that his/her previous significant other always did all of the talking, and you glean that this is a person who now feels the strong need to be *heard*, how hard will it be to make the effort to demonstrate behaviors that say, "I'm listening"? Strong eye contact, leaning in as she/he speaks, small sounds of acknowledgement, and more, are authentic behaviors that say "three of diamonds!"

And when our subject chooses that proverbial three of diamonds, everyone is happy. They have gotten exactly what they hoped to receive, and we have helped them appreciate the best qualities we have to offer. I repeat, the objective here is not to deceive anyone, not to send false signals or promise something that cannot be delivered. Instead, the idea is to identify the best parts of yourself, the parts that answer the needs of the person in front of you, and begin communicating those qualities from the moment you meet. It looks like magic, but it's really just planned common sense.

When clients come to my studio in hope of finding solutions and strategies to help them build a more successful life or career, it's required that they instantly place their trust in a total stranger. One of the quickest ways to jump that hurdle is for me to make it clear that my focus is solely on their comfort and success. They need to know I am listening and I am 100 percent engaged in finding solutions for them. There are certain body-language focal points that contribute to this feeling, and others that don't. Now, please understand, there's no attempt to fool anyone here. As a professional, I *am* committed to discovering solutions. I have every desire to be worthy of my client's trust. The point is, there are certain choices I can and must make in terms of my responses, my focus, my body language, and other elements to support this process. And the more three-of-diamond cards my client recognizes in the deck, the quicker we can get down to the work of guiding them to success.

Take a second and turn it around. If you were a customer, or the employment interviewer or the blind date or casting director, what would you want to see in the person attempting to curry your favor? How much time would you allow before the attributes you believe are essential for success in that particular situation must become evident? And wouldn't the advantage go to the candidate who was most quickly able to communicate that they are in possession of those qualities?

The magician on the stage takes absolute control over your focal points, directing you where to look and when, thus ensuring that when your focus is directed to the deck of cards, you'll see exactly what you hope to see, and hopefully rise to your feet for a standing ovation.

Think of the qualities in different situations that are required to achieve your desired result. It's not that tough. It only takes some thought and preparation. Once you identify those qualities, all you have to do is stack the deck with them.

Okay you're right, you can't get caught. Just as the magician can't get caught stuffing the rabbit into the hat. And if he gets caught, chances are, a great magician has a routine prepared making it look like you caught something you weren't supposed to see, when in fact you were intended to see it all along. Let's call that "Advanced Magic." Perhaps a bit too calculated and dependent upon misdirection for our purposes. After all, our goal here is to help you live a more authentic life, not to improve your powers of deception. Nonetheless, when you are making sure I get what I need from you, it's not helpful for you to allow me to see that you are stacking the deck with the qualities I require. So you can't get caught making me trust you; and you can't get caught practicing that sensuous tone you'll use on our first date. But the fear of being caught does not excuse you from the responsibility of making sure these qualities are evident and well-communicated because as we've learned, actions taken out of fear are never as successful as actions based upon your passion and love. Like in football, you can't play the game trying not to get hit. You play the game to win, to cross the goal line. And if you get hit, you improvise. You spin, juke, stumble, dive, whatever it takes to get you closer to the goal because that's where victory lives. In relationships, you can't spend your time trying not to offend your potential partner, avoiding revealing conversations and intimate moments in fear of exposing "something to hate." You have to put your focus on identifying and delivering the qualities your significant other most hopes to discover while still presenting your authentic self. Then you have to make them habits.

Hey, but what if you choose the wrong qualities? What if the things you guessed were most important really aren't the things your subject was hoping to see? Well, you missed. But think about it, even if you missed in choosing those qualities, you really were thinking of the other person's best interests, you still have put your focus on communicating some pretty outstanding qualities. They may not be an exact match with the expectations of your subject, but they'll still be some pretty great attributes. And chances are, those attributes will earn you more points than the self-aware, self-centered, "Me"-oriented behavior most people exhibit. You may still have a pretty good shot at the job or the relationship or the sale.

It's not magic. It's logic. And it will require some practice. But once you master the techniques any good magician practices on a daily basis, stacking the deck in your own favor to be of service to those in your circle, you will satisfy and delight your "audiences" and realize the success you deserve.

Okay, had enough rules? That should be plenty to keep you busy for a while. But I promise if you practice these techniques and employ the concepts within, you will begin to manifest more success in your life almost immediately.

Right now I'd like to give you a few small gifts in exchange for the many gifts that have been given to me. Three little secrets, let's call them, that are not so secret. Once again, they're things we all know deep down in our hearts... but we forget. We become distracted. We go against our better instincts.

In the hopes that you will remember, revitalize, and rejoice in these well-known secrets, I offer you three important things that I consider the keys to life.

You can never get enough of what you don't need to make you happy.

— Eric Hoffer

THE SECRET TO A HAPPY LIFE

We all want to be happy. And we've already addressed that the natural order of things is that we not only can be but deserve to be joyous and completely fulfilled. This incredibly beautiful world wasn't created with the idea that we should suffer and be miserable. Happiness is our birthright. The hard part is claiming it.

What's the biggest obstacle to claiming happiness? Expectation. Let's make sure we understand what we're talking about here. There's nothing wrong with expectation. We've already stated that in this life you get what you expect. But here's the catch: any of us who are dreamers and seekers have an added responsibility. We have the responsibility to not allow our aspirations to create unhappiness. In short, you're always going to be wanting more. There is no finish line. You may think at this moment that there's a certain amount of money that would make you happy or a certain promotion, award, vote of confidence or creature comfort possession that would give you the feeling you have won. But here's the bad news: there isn't. There is no amount of money you can earn that will satisfy you. As a seeker, you cannot be satisfied. You will always hunger for more. And that's a good thing. It's human nature. That's what keeps you motivated, hungry, and moving forward. But if you have the idea that there is any milestone that will satisfy you, you're going to have a really difficult time.

Let's face it, Bill Gates is still working. He continues to get up and go to an office. Is there anyone in the history of man who you would

127

think would by now have said, "I won!" This is a guy who has been listed among the top three richest people in the world for quite some time now. I think he's reported to be worth over $100 billion. There's no way on earth any one person could ever spend that kind of money. I'm sure Mr. Gates deserves every penny of the money he has earned, and I applaud him, not only for taking the steps to achieve his own personal success, but for the incredible technological contributions he has made to our society. Of even greater importance, though, is the fact that he was not satisfied. He is still working to accomplish more, earn more, and realize more success. Let's be clear here, I'm not saying Bill Gates continues to work because he is greedy and wants more and more and more. In fact, as I understand it, the majority of the work he does today is strictly charitable, making the world a better place for other people. The point is, with all of the financial success he has gained, he still wants to participate. He wants to be in the game. He wants to give back and improve the world in which he lives. As successful as he is, he is not fully satisfied. Do you honestly think if Bill Gates is not satisfied with what he has achieved, that *you* can ever reach a milestone that will make you say, "That's it, that's enough"? It's not going to happen.

And I repeat, this is a good thing. It's motivation. That's the very centerpiece of inspiration — the thoughts that drive you to continue to improve and utilize the New Rules to accomplish more and do more.

Here's the rub: you must accept and embrace the fact that you will never be satisfied, that even as the actor clutches the Oscar statuette in his or her hand, that actor is thinking, "What next?" Even when the business executive takes a company public for a personal payout of millions, the executive is thinking, "What's the next investment?" Even as the newlywed couple races down the aisle being showered with rice by friends and family, they are each thinking, "Though this is the happiest moment of my life, how can I make the next moment better?" No matter what you accomplish, as rewarding and incredible as your achievements may be, you will never be fully satisfied.

But here's the secret to life:

If we can learn to accept "I can't get no satisfaction" as a fact of life and not allow it to make us unhappy, happiness will be ours.

Our inability to be satisfied cannot equal unhappiness.

Whatever your situation right this moment, I'm sure you're hoping, wishing, and striving for more. (Yes, I concede that there are those people who are content with their place on the middle of the staircase, happy and indeed satisfied with where they are. These people are blessed — because the goal of life is happiness and contentment with their endeavors — and they probably aren't reading books on New Rules of Thinking to achieve success.) For the rest of us, maybe our bank accounts aren't what we think they should be. Maybe you don't have the job you've been hoping for or the relationship of your dreams. Maybe your car isn't the vehicle you've longed to own. Maybe you don't have a car. Whatever your situation, there is always going to be room for improvement, for upgrades… for more. But wherever you are on your journey of life, you must learn to be *happy* where you are even as you hunger for more.

This bears repeating: wherever you are on your journey of life, you must learn to be happy where you are even as you hunger for more.

Because we will never achieve satisfaction if we do not learn to be happy even as we experience dissatisfaction, and even when the goals we long to achieve seem distant, we will never be happy when we reach the milestones we have set for ourselves. I know, many of you are thinking there's no problem you have that a $1,000,000 check in the mail wouldn't solve. And it would solve a lot of problems… but it wouldn't satisfy you. You would right away begin thinking about how to parlay that million into three million. How much will taxes take? What investments might you make? What business might you open? What upgrades might you apply to your living conditions to increase the value and get you to three million? And after three million, the goal would be 10 million, or a certain award or a certain title. There is always one more dream to be realized. So there's no check coming that will satisfy you. There is no award you can receive, no title you can earn that will make you feel you have crossed the finish line. You may find ways to live more comfortably, more lavishly, even more productively, but you cannot be satisfied. You will forever want to accomplish more, create more, give more, help more, and so on. And let me remind you again, that's a good thing, as long as you can find a way to be happy where you are right now. If you can't be happy with $50 in your bank account, I promise you there will be no happiness with $50 million in your bank account. But let's also get real in the other direction. Take a second and imagine if you're really happy with $50 in your bank account, think about the fun you could have with $50 million. So what are we waiting for? Let's get busy getting happy and building our success!

The secret to a happy life is learning not to interpret hunger-for-more as a source of unhappiness. Try it. Celebrate where you are right now even as you make your plans for a brighter, richer, more success-ful future. Don't let your aspirations make you unhappy. Let them inspire you, drive you, and light the way to everything you visualize in life. Take the time to celebrate the moments in which you did reach certain goals. Keep celebrating all along the way. Happiness is yours if you allow it.

To accomplish great things,
we must dream as well as act.

— Anatole France

HOW TO ACQUIRE ANYTHING
YOU WANT IN TWO WEEKS

What do you want? What you need? You can have it. In two weeks. You don't believe me? It's true. And I'm going to share with you now how to make it happen.

People come to me all the time with problems they feel unable to solve. They need a reliable assistant; they need a new agent; they want and desire a meaningful relationship; all they need is a car they can count on. They say things like, "I've searched everywhere, and I just can't find it." "None of the companies in Los Angeles are hiring!" And so on. I always ask the obvious questions: "You've searched everywhere? *Everywhere? None* of the companies are hiring? Not one? You've approached them all with compelling evidence as to why you should be their employee?"

Usually, then, they say something like, "Well, I've approached quite a few." Or, "I sent a mailer to all of them." Unfortunately, that's not exactly the formula for acquiring something you really want.

Here comes Captain Obvious once more: the universe hates secrets. The things you want that are hidden from view, apparent only to you in the deepest recesses of your heart, have a far less chance of being realized than the things that are available for all to see. So here's the useful secret:

For the next two weeks, the first thing out of your mouth to every person you meet must be a statement of the thing you want or need. At the supermarket when the cashier says, "May I help you?" you must say, "Well, I need a reliable assistant, but until then I'd like to purchase these groceries." You think I'm kidding. I'm not.

When someone asks you how you are, your answer should be, "Well, I'd be better if I had a reliable assistant, but I'm great." Every conversation, every encounter must begin with you revealing to the universe what it is you want in your life. Consider the power of social media. Every email, post, tweet, photo, text, and other form of communication should include the phrase, "I need a reliable assistant." It can be the subject of your new YouTube video. For two weeks straight you cannot deviate from this directive. I promise you within two weeks, if the thing you want is a realistic thing of which you are deserving, it will come.

If you're wondering what the cashier at the supermarket has to do with the assistant you need, keep in mind that cashier's cousin just might be a corporate executive who has a surplus of well-trained would-be assistants. That cashier may have a son who's recently graduated business school and is looking for an opportunity. At the very least, that cashier may mention jokingly to another customer that your greeting included the need for an assistant, and the customer may say, "I know someone!"

People want to help. They want to connect good people with other good people. But if no one knows your wish, if what you desire is a well-kept secret, it will have very little chance of finding its way to you. Communicate your needs confidently, tastefully, and unobtrusively. You'll be amazed at what can happen.

For clarity's sake, obviously if what you're looking for is a long-term loving relationship, it may not always fully come to pass in two weeks. But you knew that. What we're talking about is the doorway to that realized dream. You'll be plenty satisfied if within a couple weeks you have identified the candidate for an awesome relationship. The rest is up to you; and the New Rules will help you turn that doorway into a skyscraper.

But you have to let the universe know what you want. Two weeks. Every conversation. Watch the opportunities appear.

I celebrate myself, and sing myself.

— Walt Whitman

THE FINAL SECRET

The third secret is not really a secret. It's just something we forget. Life can be challenging, tough, and sometimes confusing. The feedback and input we receive from others can surprise us, disappoint and often sadden us. The results we see from many of our actions can lead us to believe we are not winners, especially when we compare our accomplishments to others around us. At the corner newsstand, it seems magazines are created simply to give us the feeling we are "not enough." We get the sense that everyone else is more successful, richer, thinner, happier than we are. We long for our lives, our homes, and our bodies to have the same Photoshopped look those magazine cover celebrities have.

We sometimes find ourselves struggling to keep up, to get the bills paid each month, to reduce our debt, to participate fully in our careers or our relationships. And, it seems, everywhere we look there is evidence that we are powerless to realize our dreams. And even if we could make those dreams happen, we can't shake the feeling that we do not deserve the rewards connected to those lofty goals. "Who am I," we ask, "to think I deserve to live like the Joneses?"

Well, here's the third secret. It's the secret of who you are.

You are a marvel. You are a work of art. In all the universe, there is not another like you; you are an original, one of a kind. Whether you are old or young, tall or not-so-tall, heavy or thin, shaped in the image of what society has told you is beautiful or "normal," you are a gift to the world. Imperfect as you may imagine yourself to be, you, like every beautiful and magnificent sight you have ever seen, represent perfection itself.

Not because of what you have achieved; not because of your bank account, your bone structure or your intelligence, but because you are a unique, creative force impacting the entire universe with every thought and action you generate. You are a priceless masterpiece.

Take a good look at the miracle of you. Forget the measures society has taught you as to what beauty might be and what is of value. Simply look at the mechanics, the aesthetics, and the possibilities of you. What invention could you ever conceive that would outshine the marvelous invention that is you? What computer, machine, or work of art can compare to the things of which you are capable? How is it even possible a being as magnificent as yourself can exist?

You are the universe's most incredible creation.

And you are welcome on this planet. This world was created for you to co-inhabit with millions of other creatures — but there is a well-deserved place for you among them.

Here's some really good news about life: you were born to win. The world was designed for you to be happy and prosperous. Think about it.

Each morning the sun rises, illuminating the landscape and lighting our way. It warms the earth to a temperature at which we can move about addressing our daily tasks. Instinctively, the birds chirp and insects flit about pollinating plants that will become our food. The clouds give us much-needed water, the wind cools us, and the seasons change to encourage the cycles of growth and harvest. It's pretty ideal. And all of this happens without any instruction or manipulation from us. Perfection.

Without any outside direction or concentrated thinking, our hearts know to beat a certain number of beats per minute, our lungs take in oxygen, nourish our bodies and feed our blood system, and then the oxygen is converted into carbon dioxide which nourishes plant life all around us. With a single thought from the brain, our right or left arm reaches out to grasp food and place it in our mouths. And somewhere, without any need for us to know how, there is a mechanism that keeps our mouths moist, taste buds to register spices and flavors which allow us to enjoy our food, and a system that digests the food and distributes the nutrients to all the right places. Amazing! And for most of us, it's all included. It comes with our admission ticket (birth). No extra charge.

Can you see how with all of these divine systems in place functioning for our benefit, the natural order of things has to be that we are destined to be happy and prosperous? What other way could there be? It's the way it was designed. The intended order of things.

Take a moment, if you will, to observe the world in which you live. Look around you. Let go of the values placed upon how many material things you've collected, and simply observe the people, places and things within your line of vision. You'll see many of those thousands of would-be miracles that are simply part of the master plan saying you and I are meant to have a wonderful life.

I know it's hard to believe because there seem to be so many obstacles every day, but I must remind you that those obstacles are external forces, and what we're talking about here is the internal. It's the process of changing ourselves. Changing "Me" and therefore changing our experience of every single event. Taking control of the dream.

Over time, humans and animals have learned behaviors which can make us doubt our worth, our right to belong.

Never question that right.

You belong right where you are. And if you dream to inhabit a different space, with different surroundings and people, this too, is your birthright. Every day you awaken brings a new chance to begin anew, to get it "right," to learn, grow, celebrate, and bring your dreams closer to you. Why not be bold and give yourself the best chance at happiness and fulfillment? You deserve it. It is your right.

Those who would tell you that your gender, the color of your skin, the place of your birth, the shape of your body, the scores you received in school, and a thousand other qualifications are any measure of your right to the joy of living are wrong. This brief window of time is yours to savor.

Can you find ways, as the author Walt Whitman suggested at the beginning of this chapter, to celebrate yourself? There must be thousands of ways you can do that. And how might you, as Mr. Whitman continues, sing yourself? If you spent the rest of your days singing a passionate, grateful, and joyous song of you, it would still only scratch the surface of the deserved tribute to the wondrous creation that you are. Can you, will you find that song? Will you sing it at the top of your lungs for all the world to hear? Will you show the appropriate gratitude to the universe for creating such an amazing being as yourself, whose potential for happiness and success is virtually endless?

The old rules would have you believe your possibilities are limited. The New Rules will show you how your every desire is within reach when you apply them thoughtfully, morally, and uncompromisingly. It's time for a new definition of "perfection." That definition should and must include the miracle of the perfect being you are.

It all begins with "I."

Keep dreaming.

There is only one time when it is essential to awaken. That time is now.

— Buddha

ACKNOWLEDGMENTS

Although this journey began with "I," alone at a wooden desk at the Rancho Mirage Public Library, it certainly could not have come together without the brilliance, generosity, patience, and encouragement of some very special individuals.

I have always believed that one must choose wisely the people from whom one accepts advice, and this choice may be among the smartest things I have ever done. I owe a great deal of gratitude to my "team of advisors" who selflessly agreed at a moment's notice to read, take notes on, and compassionately give impressions and corrections about numerous chapters, false starts, rewrites, and failed attempts. Teddi Silverman, Brother Chris Saindon, Maureen Robinson, Richard Baum, and Claudia Sloan were powerfully fearless in asserting their feeling as to which concepts authentically supported the message I passionately set out to communicate. They were equally insightful and diplomatic in sharing their views, and were most always 100 percent on the mark. For this, I am hugely grateful.

My students, clients, and friends were extremely generous in supporting the idea to complete this book, and their unwavering spirit is reflected on every page within. I offer my gratitude to my business partners Judy Rich and Pat Brannon as well as Cory Bertisch, Jamie Bertisch, Randy J Bertisch and the entire team at My Gym Enterprises for their patience and support as I juggled responsibilities while completing this project.

For many years I have been advised that I should create a book based upon the topics within my speaking engagements and seminars, and yet I was never able to make it happen until I received the urging, the belief, and the deadlines offered by my manager and friend, Linda Ballew. Thank you.

My distributors Molly and Aaron Silverman invested time, belief, and support long before common sense would have dictated, as did my publicist Leshelle Sargent, my digital media strategist Brandon Aristotle Lucas, and my web designer Daniel Mullenix. Thank you, Kara Kenna, Janis Uhley and Janna Wong for making the finished book correct and beautiful.

I have been warned by many wise people never to mix business and friendship. Fortunately, the New Rules of Thinking taught me to ignore that advice unless adding the word "badly" at the end. In choosing a publisher, I could not have done it any better. Claudia Sloan has been so much more than a publisher; she became my editor, proofreader, coach, ghost writer, support system and more while continuing to be the dearest of friends through grueling late-night sessions and deadlines. She is, in short, a miracle worker... and there are not enough thanks to do justice to her contribution.

Finally, without the support of my incredible family, and my wonderful group of longtime friends — the WTF club - this could never have been accomplished. My inspiration continues to come from my children, Nicolette K. Robinson, Ally K. Robinson, and Leslie Odom Jr. Without the spark they provide, these New Rules would never have been created, employed, or proven to lead to the incredible life I live.

Before the first word was committed to paper, my wife and best friend, Maureen Robinson, willingly accepted the role of catalyst, inspiration, champion, business partner and therapist. Her contribution to this book is immeasurable.

Her unwavering belief, dedication, and effort made most everything possible, and her relentless commitment to the success of this project inspired every chapter, page, and word.

ABOUT THE AUTHOR

Stuart K Robinson is a unique motivational speaker who has inspired audiences around the world with his life-changing "New Rules of Thinking." As a coach and corporate consultant, Stuart K has inspired many through his Robinson Creative Lab where he works with people from all walks of life guiding them to become more effective in their careers, relationships, and personal goals.

Stuart's powerful message carries into his role as CEO and co-owner of one of the top talent agencies in Hollywood. Stuart K is also widely regarded as among the most sought-after acting instructors/career coaches in the nation.

Over many years in the entertainment industry, Stuart — an award-winning director, actor, singer/composer and writer — has been seen in movies and television shows with Sylvester Stallone, Charles Bronson, Cicily Tyson, Ted Danson, John Cusack, Jack Klugman and William Shatner, to name a few, and has appeared in more than 100 TV commercials.

As an in-demand director, Stuart K has helmed productions for PBS, the Disney Channel, Off-Broadway, and a recent production in Washington D.C. where the keynote speaker was President Barack Obama.

He also serves as Executive Vice President, Creative/Brand Extension for My Gym Enterprises, a worldwide corporation which franchises over 340 children's fitness centers around the globe.

NOTES ABOUT "I"

NOTES ABOUT "I"

NOTES ABOUT "I"

NOTES ABOUT "I"

NOTES ABOUT "I"